KINGDOM
PRAYER

KINGDOM
PRAYER

*Touching Heaven
to Change Earth*

Tony Evans

MOODY PUBLISHERS

CHICAGO

© 2016 by
ANTHONY T. EVANS

Unless otherwise indicated, Scripture quotations are from the New American Standard Bible®, Copyright © 1960, 1962, 1963, 1968, 1971, 1972, 1973, 1975, 1977, 1995 by The Lockman Foundation. Used by permission. (www.Lockman.org)

Scripture quotations marked NIV are taken from the Holy Bible, New International Version®, NIV®. Copyright © 1973, 1978, 1984, 2011 by Biblica, Inc.™ Used by permission of Zondervan. All rights reserved worldwide. www.zondervan.com. The "NIV" and "New International Version" are trademarks registered in the United States Patent and Trademark Office by Biblica, Inc.™

Scripture quotations marked NKJV are taken from the New King James Version. Copyright © 1982 by Thomas Nelson. Used by permission. All rights reserved.

All websites listed herein are accurate at the time of publication but may change in the future or cease to exist. The listing of website references and resources does not imply publisher endorsement of the site's entire contents. Groups and organizations are listed for informational purposes, and listing does not imply publisher endorsement of their activities.

Edited by: Jim Vincent
Interior and Cover design: Erik M. Peterson

Library of Congress Cataloging-in-Publication Data

Names: Evans, Tony, 1949- author.
Title: Kingdom prayer : touching heaven to change earth / Tony Evans.
Description: Chicago : Moody Publishers, 2016.
Identifiers: LCCN 2016028231 (print) | LCCN 2016031683 (ebook) | ISBN 9780802414847 | ISBN 9780802494771 ()
Subjects: LCSH: Prayer--Christianity.
Classification: LCC BV210.3 .E935 2016 (print) | LCC BV210.3 (ebook) | DDC 248.3/2--dc23
LC record available at https://lccn.loc.gov/2016028231

ISBN: 978-0-8024-1484-7

We hope you enjoy this book from Moody Publishers. Our goal is to provide high-quality, thought-provoking books and products that connect truth to your real needs and challenges. For more information on other books and products written and produced from a biblical perspective, go to www.moodypublishers.com or write to:

Moody Publishers
820 N. LaSalle Boulevard
Chicago, IL 60610

1 3 5 7 9 10 8 6 4 2

Printed in the United States of America

Contents

Why Is Praying a Challenge?

If the truth be told, prayer is hard work. While all serious Christians recognize the importance that the Bible places on prayer, most fall short when it comes to doing it. I must confess that it is a lot easier for me as a pastor to preach about prayer than to spend that same amount of time engaged in it.

As a pastor I am also aware of how much easier it is to draw a crowd for a special sermon, special guest speaker, or program than it is for a prayer meeting. Even when there is a determination to pray, distractions seem to always show up. The mind wanders, people interrupt, and I, like you, often fall asleep early in the process. We feel guilty, commit to do better, but after a while fall back into the same old prayer struggle of neglect or routine prayers.

This naturally raises the central question: Why is something so strategic to the Christian life, our relationship with God, and victory in life such a challenge? The answer is that prayer links us to a realm we are unfamiliar navigating. Paul calls it "heavenly places." Prayer is the God-given communication link between heaven and earth, time and eternity, the finite and the infinite.

Because the enemy of our souls knows how unfamiliar we are with operating consistently in the spiritual realm, he also knows we quickly revert back to what the five senses are comfortable with. After all, when we pray, we are talking to someone who we can't see and who is not audibly talking back to us. This causes some of us to feel like we often are musing aimlessly in thin air.

When we come to realize, however, that prayer is the divinely authorized means to access the kingdom of heaven and to get that kingdom to intervene in the affairs of our earthly life, it affects both our perception of and persistence in prayer. I define kingdom prayer as *the divinely authorized methodology to access heavenly authority for earthly intervention*. Prayer is God's backstage pass into a personal audience with Him. Thus the enemy, not wanting us to make contact, seeks to divert our belief, confidence, determination, and our practice of prayer. Prayer, unlike anything else, grants us legitimate authority to invoke heaven into history, so that God is welcomed into our affairs.

This explains why God allows negative events into our lives that we can't fix, forcing us to pursue Him in prayer out of the desperation of our circumstances. I was reminded of this truth when I watched the movie *War Room*. To save her marriage and family, Elizabeth Jordan (played by Pricilla Shirer, my daughter) turned her closet into a place of focused, concentrated prayer. She came to realize only heaven could fix what earth couldn't. When we truly come to realize that much of God's activity in history is determined by the presence or absence of prayer, then fighting through the distractions becomes a lot more effective.

My goal in *Kingdom Prayer* is to confront you afresh with the untapped power and authority that we have in prayer and to motivate you and me to utilize our backstage pass to access our heavenly father for our deepest needs.

So I invite you to join me in giving God permission and an invitation for earthly intervention; an intervention that is essential if we are to experience victory in our personal lives, families, churches, and communities.

PART 1

The Concept of Kingdom Prayer

CHAPTER 1

Power and Promises

A number of years ago, I took the family on a vacation to see one of the great wonders of the world. We had already been to the Grand Canyon and gotten to *ooh* and *ahh* about the scenery there. Personally, I didn't completely understand why we had to drive that far to see a hole in the ground, but it was on the list of "Great Family Vacation Destinations" so we went.

This vacation, we went to see another hole in the ground— or what looked like a hole in the ground from up above. The difference, though, was that this hole was filled with an enormous amount of water. It didn't take me more than one look to understand why we had come. It was overpowering in its beauty. I couldn't look away.

Niagara Falls proved to be a great adventure for us as a family, but as we spent a few days there, something else stood out to me about the experience in relationship to prayer and our experience of God Himself.

We had chosen to stay on the Canadian side of the Falls for our vacation, and so when we had arrived at our hotel room the first night, that became our initial opportunity to see the mammoth horseshoe-carved landmark, flooded with an on-going surge of water causing it to be soaked with foam at the bottom. I'll never forget looking out the window of our hotel room that very first time and being overwhelmed by the magnificence of this natural wonder. It seemed close. It seemed enormous. I recall mouthing the word "wow" and just standing at the big window with the family, staring in amazement. We were all impressed at the majesty flowing in front of us.

But it was too late that evening to actually go and visit Niagara Falls up close. Instead, we unpacked, grabbed some dinner, and went to bed. The next morning, Lois and I woke the kids and headed out to show them a closer, more powerful view. We headed out the hotel, went down a walkway, and then took a short ride on a hillside tram to get to a little park and visitor area right at the top of the Falls.

Now, the view from our room had been spectacular. There were no complaints mumbled at all. But the view from the park area right where the water literally lunges over the edges of stone and rock—well, that view was breathtaking. I didn't just mouth one "wow" like in the hotel room. This time as I stood there witnessing the immeasurable amount of water nose-diving off the rim of the upper riverbed, I voiced my amazement out loud. Several times. The thunderous roar of the water hitting the basin never stopped. The rainbow painted in the sky shone above it, immovable—almost like a sentry positioned on duty.

We stood there bathed in the constant sound and sight of pure wonder. If you've been there yourself, you know we also got a little wet as the water's spray would fly through the air, sprinkling us as it went about its way.

Witnessing the Falls firsthand—close enough to feel as if I

could reach out and touch it—evoked a profound sense of awe within me. Hours went by in what seemed like only minutes.

But there is a third way to experience Niagara Falls, one many visitors on the Falls' American side enjoy. It's called the Maid of the Mist, a magnificent boat you can ride close to the foot of the Falls. If you have been on it yourself then you know that the word "mist" is an understatement. When you ride the Maid of the Mist, you don't get misted at all. You get drenched. But "Maid of the Drench" probably wouldn't go over as well in marketing the riverboat ride!

Everyone is given a raincoat before they board the boat. This is intentional because the owners of the boat know you are about to get really wet. Before long, the cold, penetrating river water that just fell fifty-seven meters (one hundred eighty-seven feet) from the cliffs at Niagara soaks everyone on board. Passengers on the boat don't merely see the Falls. They don't merely hear them. They don't merely get sprinkled with droplets on the breeze. No, on that boat they are drenched as they experience Niagara as close as is humanly possible without actually going over it in one of those barrels that many adventurous daredevils have tried.

CLOSE, CLOSER, CLOSEST

These three very different experiences offered visitors to Niagara Falls reminded me of our relationship to prayer and our experience of God Himself. Some of us approach our prayer lives and relational experience of God from the hotel room of our hearts. We see Him from a distance. Yes, we are duly impressed, but not really impacted. We admire His work from afar but then we become easily distracted because it's just an image out a window. We might mouth a word or two. But before long we have turned to do other things, or simply gotten bored with the view.

Then there are others of us who engage our prayer lives from the park. We're closer. We abide a bit more. We stay a little longer. But we are still safely behind the steel and rock barriers of our own will and minds. We don't allow the current to connect with us or direct us in any way. Yes, we may feel His engagement and hear His voice, like answers blown to us on the breeze, but then there are other times where we become easily distracted by the visitor center souvenirs to purchase, or the hamburgers, ice cream, and pretzels nearby. Before long, we've left His presence and entered the store.

But there are some who refuse to settle for a hotel room window or even park experience of prayer. They are the ones who put on their raincoats, raise their umbrellas, and venture into the basin to get as close as they can. They long to be drenched by God's presence. Drenched by His purity. Overwhelmed by His glory. They see not just the rainbow of His promises but move into the actual light of His promises. They may get uncomfortable sometimes as the boat gets rocky or they get drenched, but it's worth it as they fully engage with the One who truly is the voice on the waters. As the psalmist writes, "The voice of the Lord is upon the waters; the God of glory thunders, the Lord is over many waters," (Ps. 29:3). That is the voice you hear, know, and experience. And with His voice comes His power.

Did you know that Niagara Falls is not only a spectacle of wonder to behold? It is also a source of power, great power. In fact, a fourth of all of New York State as well as Ontario are powered by these falls alone. The Niagara generating stations create hydropower that can turn on 24 million 100-watt light bulbs at one time. There is nothing quite like Niagara Falls in physically illustrating a spiritual principle with regard to prayer. Both promises (the rainbows) and power (enormous hydroelectricity) come from this one place.

But it is up to you whether you choose to simply view the postcard or the calendar photo featuring the Niagara Falls. You could go a step further and take a trip to a hotel close to the Falls and look out the window. Or you could choose to make the walk down to the park and line up at the edge where the water cascades for a closer look. *Or* if you will decide to go all the way—put on the raincoat, get on the boat, and be drenched by both the power and promises of that place.

It's your choice. But while you do get to make your choice, you don't get to choose the outcomes of that choice. The choice itself will influence the results. If you want the full power and promises of God's presence, you will have to get close and go deep in your relationship with Him.

TRUE POWER

Prayer has been studied, written about, talked about, and preached on by countless people in countless ways. Yet it remains an elusive element to most of us. In over four decades of ministry, I have encountered only a few who truly seem to grasp and understand prayer. For far too many people, even those who follow Jesus Christ, prayer is like the National Anthem before a sporting event. It gets the game going but has little to no relevance on what is happening on the field. It is merely an exercise of routine.

For example, when most of us pray before we eat, we don't really utilize our minds to do that because we say the same general things each time. Or when many of us pray before we go to bed at night, we simply recite a call for blessing and protection with a little bit of gratitude thrown in for good measure.

Prayer has become a habit for far too many of us.

Yet prayer is powerful. Kingdom prayer is *the divinely authorized methodology to access heavenly authority for earthly intervention.* Such prayer is earth giving heaven permission to intervene in the reality down here with the manifestation of the spiritual reality up there. That is a definition few of us really grasp. God is waiting to be involved in our activities and yet because we were given freedom He does not force Himself on our situations. He waits for us to ask—to connect with Him in prayer.

There was a lady who lived way out in the boondocks for years without any electricity, but finally the power company was able to get electricity installed where she lived. But after several months, the power company noticed that very little power was being used at this woman's home. They did some tests and saw that the power was getting to her house just fine, but she didn't seem to be using much at all. So a representative decided to visit her home and ask if there was a problem.

> *God does not force Himself on our situations. He waits for us to ask—to connect with Him in prayer.*

"Ma'am, are you using your electricity here that we've run to your property?" he asked.

"Oh, yes!" she replied. "It's been very helpful."

"Can you explain to me how you use your new electric power?"

"Well, it's very simple," she said. "When it begins to get dark,

I turn on the lights long enough to light my kerosene lamps and then I turn the lights off again."

I'm sure you will agree with me this lady didn't understand the use of the power. She had it, but she wasn't maximizing it; she wasn't getting all of the power that it was designed to deliver. It's the same way with prayer. In order to experience maximum spiritual power, we need to understand how this thing called prayer is designed to work.

We sing songs about power. Our songs remind us of all of the deposits that God has made in us, yet so many of us are living as though we are powerless. Now, how can you live in God's prayer power? It starts by first knowing Him—really being intimate with who God is. Being willing to get drenched on the boat and take a trip into the basin of God's presence. Now, that doesn't mean how many Bible verses you have memorized or how many theological concepts you have mastered. Those academic pursuits have their place, but knowing God personally in prayer is more than that. When you become intimate with God, it's not a vague concept—it's an ongoing conversation. It's an experiential reality that produces results.

FINDING POWER BEFORE WE "LOSE HEART"

When you experience God the way He intended, you will experience power in your prayers like never before. The apostle Paul introduces this concept when he makes the statement in my favorite New Testament book, Ephesians, "Therefore I ask you not to lose heart" (3:13). To "lose heart" means to become discouraged, despondent, and finally, to give up. There is a lot today to lose heart over. It might be a financial situation, a relationship, a health concern, loss of a job, or emotional distress. Just watching the evening news can cause anyone to lose heart very quickly.

So much that surrounds us today speaks of doom, gloom, and unfortunate situations. As a pastor, I am regularly called on to counsel people. There isn't a week—and often even a day—that passes when I do not speak with someone who is ready to give up.

Paul must have heard many similar accounts. And his concern for the believers at Ephesus—"saints" as he called them (so they were saved people)—was that they would not lose heart. This concern thus led Paul to pray one of the great prayers of the New Testament. This prayer for power, found in Ephesians 3:14–19, is often overlooked when it comes to Bible study, but I believe it to be one of the most insightful and powerful models of prayer that has been given to us.

PAUL'S PRAYER FOR OUR POWER

In verse 14, Paul writes, "For this reason I bow my knees before the Father, from whom every family in heaven and on earth derives its name." Now understand: When the Bible mentions that somebody has dropped down to their knees, it means this-is-serious-prayer time. This was a humbling kind of prayer.

Paul continues with this mighty prayer. He prays that God "would grant you, according to the riches of His glory, to be strengthened with power through His Spirit in the inner man" (v. 16). Paul is basically asking that God would give the Ephesian believers some power. But what kind of power is Paul referring to? He's talking about power to no longer allow your circumstances to own you. He's talking about the power to deal with a losing-heart situation. He's talking to weak people who need to be strengthened because of what they are going through.

They don't have the power to get out of the situation, or even through it, by themselves. They cannot overcome the circumstance, deal with the pain, or find the answer. They feel so powerless that they are losing heart. That is the context in which Paul prays this prayer.

Through his prayer, Paul is saying to them—and to you and me—that the answer is not on the outside. It's not found in changing the situation. Paul is saying the power to not succumb to losing heart is based on the Spirit's work *inside* of you.

Many of us who are losing heart try to change the external situation. We don't think to make an adjustment on the inside, where real change can take place. This only makes us more frustrated. And then we wonder why there's no power and nothing happening.

Have you ever picked up your cellphone only to notice there is no power left in it? It powers down and now you can't access your contacts or even dial a number. You can't call out and no one can call in because there is an absence of power.

When this happens, you or I could scream at our phones and say, "Come on, someone talk to me!" But that wouldn't change anything. We could push the screen harder or shake the phone. We could say nice words to it or look at it longingly. Yet still nothing would change. Nothing would turn it on—except simply plugging it in. All efforts are doomed to failure and frustration unless something got charged in the inner casing.

Many of us who are losing heart in our physical, tangible lives and experiences are making ourselves more frustrated by trying to change the external situations and dynamics when there has been no adjustment on the internal connection. Then we wonder why there is no power and nothing seems to be happening.

Here is what Paul had to say about situations like this in Ephesians 3:16–18 (NIV):

> I pray that out of his glorious riches he may strengthen you with power through his Spirit in your inner being, so that Christ may dwell in your hearts through faith. And I pray that you, being rooted and established in love, may have power, together with all the Lord's holy people, to grasp how wide and long and high and deep is the love of Christ.

The Greek word "dwell" means to make yourself at home. That's a key word to understanding the power of prayer. Let me illustrate it through this comparison. Many of us have a welcome sign outside of our front door. When someone comes to our home, we say "Come in! Make yourself at home." But let's face it—we don't usually mean that. Rather, it's just something polite that we say to welcome a guest. It would be more correct to say, "Make yourself at *room*," because we don't really mean that a guest can wander throughout our entire home. They can't go into your bedroom or peek into your closets. Those areas are private. They are off-limits.

MAKING JESUS WELCOME IN OUR LIVES

Likewise, most of us have "Jesus places" in our lives. These are the areas of our lives where Jesus is welcome to enter. Those parts of our lives that are tidy and clean. But if you want real spiritual power, Jesus needs to be able to enter *all* the rooms in your house. He must be free to make Himself at home. You need to let Him in the dirty garage or the overflowing attic. You need to let him in the closets. You might be asking why this is. It's because Jesus will only address what He has access to.

We call this the lordship of Jesus Christ, which is giving Christ access to the ownership, rulership, over every place of your life. In order for Jesus to be Lord of your life, He must be invited to integrate throughout all of it—not just come for a visit on Sunday morning at church. You must allow Him to roam freely in every nook and cranny of your daily thoughts, needs, desires, despairs, and more. If you give Jesus Christ limited access to and engagement with you, you can expect to have limited power from Him. And limited power from Christ means more "losing heart" when the trials of life come our way as well as weak, anemic prayers.

For instance, you invite Jesus to Sunday morning church. It's a big room He has been invited to. But after your church service is over and you have driven home, you let Him into your home's entryway but not into any of the rooms. And that's why you can be one way at church and another way in your car. It's as if you are saying, "Church is Your room, but my home and its rooms are mine."

But Jesus must be free in our inner person to dwell there, to make Himself at home rather than just drop by at the threshold of our home and a couple of hours at church. The reason Jesus needs to be free to roam is so that you can know the breadth, the length, the height, and the depth of His love, just as Ephesians 3:17–19 says. And even when you come to know all of that, you will only be scratching the surface.

THE DEPTH OF HIS POWER IN US

I'll never forget watching the enormous amount of water pour continually over the Niagara Falls. Over and over and over again, it never stopped. While we slept in our hotel room, it still poured. While we went and ate lunch somewhere, it still poured. In time, I began to be more impressed with why the basin didn't begin to fill up and overflow like a bathtub with its faucet left to run. How did this relatively still-watered basin continue to absorb such a mammoth amount of water and remain at the same capacity? The answer to that is found in its depth. See, the basin at the foot of the Falls is as deep as the Falls is high. Both measure exactly fifty-seven meters. So when you see the water dumping into the relatively small looking area beneath the cliffs, it is going much deeper than you may have realized—look at its awesome height and realize its depth is just as great. This space allows the water the space it needs to keep coming at such a great pace.

When you are tied into Christ and His love for you, He creates the depth you need to receive the enormous amount of power God has to provide you through prayer. On your own, it would be too much. But when you dwell with Christ, His depth becomes your own and you will experience a whole new level of spiritual capacity.

God is inexhaustible and infinite, which means He has no concluding point. To give you a point of reference, look at how long man has been on the earth. In all that time, no one has ever made the trip to the end of the galaxy we are in. We don't even know *where* our galaxy ends. Sure, we've made a trip to the moon and landed space craft on Mars, but with all of the thousands of years mankind has been here, we are still trying to figure out what's in our own galaxy. And that's just *our* galaxy. We know that there are many more galaxies out there. And God created every single galaxy that exists. Just thinking on that makes it easier to realize how awesome God truly is.

Or let's consider our sun, which is ninety-three million miles from Earth. If you were to rocket at 17,000 miles per hour (the average speed of a manned space craft orbiting around the earth) to the sun without stopping for any breaks, it would take seven and one-half months to make the trip.[1] More than seven months just to get there, and yet our sun provides us with the daily, hourly life-giving supply of energy that our earth and its inhabitants need to survive. And it does so immediately, each second of the day. (Traveling at the speed of light, the sun's bright rays reach us in about eight minutes.)

I'm trying to help you understand who we're dealing with. Clearly, this mighty God is beyond our comprehension. He is higher than we can see, reaches deeper than we can dive, and is wider than we can wrap our arms around.

But the good news is that God isn't looking for His children to have academic knowledge of Who He is. What He wants us to have is the capacity to experience Him, "to know the love of Christ which surpasses knowledge" (Eph. 3:19), to experience the reality of Him operating without limit in our lives through this process called prayer.

Friend, you may be losing heart. You may be tired or even discouraged. But Paul is telling us that being rooted and grounded in the love of Jesus will fill us up with all the fullness of God. When God is allowed to dwell in *all* of the rooms of your heart—when His power is allowed to freely flow within you like the water over the Niagara—you will be connected to a Source that provides more power and promises that you could ever even imagine possible. This is what kingdom prayer is all about.

CHAPTER 2

Authority and Access

I n more than four decades of ministry, I have found that far too many people don't understand one key principle of kingdom living and kingdom authority—*prayer*. Prayer is a critical principle, vital to the Christian walk. It's so much more than just voicing our requests to God as though He's waiting in heaven to take our orders.

The moment we accepted Jesus as our Savior, we were given the privilege of entering God's holy presence. Jesus, with full authority as God's Son, now escorts us into the kingdom throne room. I've never been in a throne room of a living king on earth, but even without having visited one I know that inside such a room rests an inordinate amount of power and authority. One word, command, or statement from the ruler, and it is done. Something you won't hear in any royal throne room is the phrase, "But, King?" Instead, you hear, "Yes, your majesty."

This is because the role itself demands obedience.

Thus when we are given, through Christ, the freedom to enter the throne room of God in our prayers, we should never take that lightly. We are entering into the presence of the One whose rule is over all. What He says goes. What He determines is final.

In chapter 1 we defined kingdom prayer as *the divinely authorized methodology to access heavenly authority for earthly intervention*. Yet even though prayer is such a powerful tool, many believers struggle with it. Sometimes prayer can feel like putting four quarters in a soda machine, pushing the button, and not getting any response at all. You push the button again and again; you even nudge it with your foot. But still, nothing happens, leaving you to eventually walk away feeling frustrated.

Because of this, I believe that prayer is the most underused source of accessing spiritual authority that God has given us. It is not underused due to its inability to function as God intended but rather due to our lack of understanding and application of how it works—and *why* it was designed in the first place. Kingdom prayer is the established mechanism to advance God's kingdom agenda on earth by accessing His authority in heaven and drawing it down. In this way, His rule is advanced in history.

KINGDOM PRAYER
IS ABOUT AUTHORITY

Kingdom prayer is all about authority. Yet we rarely think of it that way. Prayer is one of the most important and effective things we can do as believers. Yet we rarely approach it that way. That is why I set out to compile my teachings on this subject into this book. Examining the authoritative nature of prayer, its relationship to God's kingdom, as well as the DNA of effective prayer will be my emphasis in this book—much more than the mechanics of how to do it.

I would never teach someone how to talk to another person

or where to talk to another person. So I'm not going to focus on how or where you talk to God. The how of prayer—how it is done, where it is done, when it is done—is up to you based on your relational intimacy with the Lord. The time of day is unimportant, but the frequency is. We should pray often. After all, Paul tells us to pray without ceasing (1 Thess. 5:16). By that statement alone, the *how* of prayer will have to come in a variety of ways and places. Prayer is about so much more than a routine, location, length of time, or even the exact words that we use.

Remember, Peter prayed just three words when sinking under the waves in a storm, "Lord, save me!" They weren't eloquent words. He was on waves, not in a prayer closet. He wasn't kneeling; he was sinking. And he didn't even bother to exalt God with a long list of attributes or open with a song. Rather, he cried out in a heart of both authenticity and need, and he was heard. The heart of prayer often speaks louder than the words.

KINGDOM PRAYER
IS HONEST COMMUNICATION

Prayer is relational communication with God. It is sincere, direct, and honest. Just as Peter spoke to Jesus on the water, we are to speak to Him ourselves. Open your mouth and pray. Don't worry so much about how you do it or even what you say—just start. Because prayer is a form of communication, it comes in a myriad of formats. It can happen while you are driving, while you are sitting in a meeting, during a conversation you are having with your spouse, or even while you may be watching sports on the TV—just drop the volume, close your eyes, and approach the King of heaven with the deep issue now brought to your mind. You don't have to get down on your knees each and every time you pray. You don't have to hang your halo above your head, pull out your twenty-pound prayer journal, and throw in words like "Thou" and "Thee."

But you do have to be honest. You have to be real with God. Humility is good as well, a key quality that we will explore in this book. But the moment you begin to think that prayer is to be carried out as a program, in order to check it off your list—that's the moment you will lose access to the power and authority it contains.

Communicating with God is not a program. Communicating with God is *communicating with God*.

Now, let me clarify. Am I saying that kneeling is wrong? No, of course not. I kneel and have knelt beside my bed to pray for decades, regularly. Am I saying that prayer journals are wrong? Again, no. If that's what you use to remind you of how God has worked in your life before as well as to record what you are seeking from Him now, by all means use it. Is a private, isolated area—a prayer closet—bad? No, it's a great place to pray. Scripture tells us to pray quietly alone where no one can see. There are times we are told to pray in our inner rooms (Matt. 6:6).

> *The ingredients of effective prayer include faith, authority, surrender, obedience, tenacity, and trust.*

It's just that there are other times we are told to pray publicly as well (1 Tim. 2:8). The inner room is not the only place to pray. Remember Peter, thrashing around on the waves, chose a very good place to pray. We know this because his prayer was answered.

Rather than get caught up in the rules and the do's and the don'ts of praying . . . since they vary by as many situations of life, I want us to look at the spirit behind prayer, the DNA of what makes it work—things like faith, alignment, authority, surrender, obedience, tenacity, trust, and love. These are the ingredients of effective prayer. And effective prayer is what you and I need because we are in a battle, in the midst of a spiritual battle between good and evil. And prayer is our primary weapon for victory.

PRAY ALWAYS . . .

The apostle Paul gave us one of the great secrets for powerful kingdom prayer, especially related to this area of spiritual warfare. After instructing us to put on the full armor of God in Ephesians 6, he wrote, "With all prayer and petition pray at all times in the Spirit, and with this in view, be on the alert with all perseverance and petition for all the saints" (v. 18).

Notice how many times Paul used the word "pray" or a synonym for prayer in that one verse. It appears as (1) "all prayer," (2) "petition," and (3) "prayer."

Even though Paul had just completed explaining the weapons of spiritual warfare and how they work, he chose to wind up his talk on that subject by looking at prayer. He culminated his strategy session on spiritual battles with this one powerful method of repeated, constant, persevering, all-encompassing prayer. "All prayer . . . petition . . . pray at all times."

. . . AND LISTEN TO HIM

God longs to communicate with you—to listen to what you have to say. He also wants you to listen for His voice, to know

His voice and abide with Him. The correct image of God to keep in mind as you think about strengthening your personal prayer life is that He's vitally interested in you and your prayers. And He desires for you to be vitally interested in hearing from Him. He wants you to pray always, at all times for the simple reason that He wants heaven to stay connected to earth through you.

What's more, once you begin to hear and discern God's voice in your ongoing fellowship with Him and through His Word, it is as satisfying as anything you could ever experience. He is as close a friend as you will ever know. He will guide you, direct you, comfort you, surprise you, and even spoil you with His love. He can also deepen your wisdom with His insight so you can avoid wrong decisions and enjoy the fruit of right ones. He can even open up doors where they had previously been locked shut.

I'll never forget when the kids were younger and Lois and I took them to the Grand Canyon. We'd driven all day in order to save on travel expenses, and by the time we got there it was pretty late. We arrived tired and ready to head to our hotel room to go to sleep. Yet there was one fairly major problem. I had forgotten to reserve us a room.

Keep in mind this was about thirty years ago. Before cell-phones were common, before the Internet existed. We had made it to the Grand Canyon and the official hotel on site. But it was already full. The hotel manager even told me that there was a waiting list in case any rooms became available. No other hotels were within an hour or so. The situation looked bleak.

Worn out, hungry, and frustrated, I decided we would sit down as a family and have a meal before making the long drive to try and find another hotel. When we sat down to dinner, Priscilla—a small child at the time—asked, "Daddy, didn't you teach us that God will provide all of our needs?"

Trust me, I was in no mood to have one of my children point out what Daddy had preached on a Sunday. So I gave her one of those daddy looks that said, "Priscilla, be quiet and get ready to eat your meal."

"DADDY, WHY DON'T YOU PRAY?"

But Priscilla continued. "Daddy, if God is going to provide all of our needs and all we need to do is ask Him, then why don't you pray?" She looked at me with an innocence in her eyes that was touching. It was one of those moments when, as a father, you want to crawl under the table because your child is being more spiritual than you are. It was also one of those moments when I didn't feel at all like praying. So I told her, "You pray, Priscilla." She did. Loud enough for the people around us also eating dinner to hear.

After Priscilla's prayer, I started thinking about how I would explain to her that God doesn't always instantly come through when we pray. But things never got that far, because not long after Priscilla's prayer, the hotel manager came to our table and asked me if we still needed a room. I nodded yes.

"Well," he said, "one of our guests just had a medical emergency and had to leave—and the next family on the waiting list has already left. So we have a room for you if you want it."

Priscilla smiled a huge smile. I just shook my head and said, "Wow." Prayer *is* a powerful tool because prayer *is* communicating with the all-powerful God who longs to execute His authority to and through us but only as we give Him permission to do so through prayer. Unfortunately, many of us have simply "outgrown" it. More precisely, we have outgrown the childlike faith that believes God will do what He says He will.

One key to prayer is having faith like a child—as Priscilla modeled for me so many years ago. Another is knowing what you ought to pray. A third is understanding that prayer is authoritative in nature, when based on the power and truth of God attached to His kingdom purposes.

THE DOMINION MANDATE

To grasp the authoritative nature of prayer, we need to go back to the beginning of human time. It is in the context of our creation that we come to fully understand the authority we hold within prayer. Let's start where all things started at the time when "God created the heavens and the earth. The earth was formless and void, and darkness was over the surface of the deep" (Gen. 1:1–2).

In succession God separated light from darkness (v. 4), sky from water (v. 7), and the land from the sea (v. 9). Subsequently He created vegetation, the celestial lights (including the sun and the moon), marine, bird, and animal life, and finally human life. When God created man and woman He chose to create a lesser creature—an inferior being, constitutionally less than the angels (Ps. 8:5; Heb. 2:7 NIV). He did this for many reasons, but one purpose was that this creature (humanity) would demonstrate what God could do with us when we are fully dependent upon Him.

Recall that God had ejected Satan from heaven when he attempted to usurp His throne and rule, casting the devil and a third of the angels who had followed him to Earth (see Isa. 14:12–15; Ezek. 28:16–17; Rev. 12:4).

Thus God set forth to create the human race in order to rule over His created order. We see this in Psalm 8, as David wrote:

> When I consider Your heavens, the work of Your fingers, the moon and the stars, which You have ordained; what is man, that You are mindful of him, and the son of man, that You visit him? For You have made him a little lower than the angels, and You crown him with glory and honor. You have made him to have dominion over the works of Your hands; You have put all things under his feet. (vv. 3–6 NKJV)

This is why, when God created Adam and Eve, He said, "Let them rule over the fish of the sea and over the birds of the sky and over the cattle and over all the earth" (Gen.1:26). Then God told them to "subdue" the earth (v. 28). This is known in theological terms as the *dominion covenant,* or the *dominion mandate.*

In other words, it was impossible that God would not have a kingdom that would rule over and defeat the kingdom of Satan. When Jesus Christ sets up His millennial kingdom, it will be the final, triumphant declaration of God's glory. Satan will then be chained up during that time to demonstrate his utter defeat and judgment (see Rev. 20:1–3).

Yet, for now, God has created you and me to harness and rule a part of His creation. Every person was created with that divine intent. Why is it important for you to grasp the unfolding of God's kingdom plan, especially with regard to the subject of prayer? Because when God said, "Let them rule," He stated that He would not rule independently of man—mankind's decisions would now carry weight regarding what He did or did not do. And He did this for one reason—to demonstrate to the devil and the demons that He could do more through a lesser creature in manifesting His glory than through the once shining "star of the morning" (Isa. 14:12).

A Cosmic Conflict

Numbers of people think that there is a battle going on between God and the devil. You may think so yourself. Yet there is no battle going on between God and the devil. If there was, it wouldn't last long. That's like saying, "Tony Evans and Manny Pacquiao are fighting." Sure, we might both climb into the ring together to have it out, but I would be no match for "Pac-Man."

Satan, a created creature, is no match for the omnipotent Creator. That's not even a fight. But what God did do was create humanity, who by ourselves are not on even competitive terms with Satan or his demons, to demonstrate that in this spiritual battle even the inferior creature can win when he or she operates according to God's governance, authority, and kingdom rule.

You and I were cast in a cosmic conflict to manifest God's rule in history for the advancement of His kingdom and the reflection of His glory. One majestic way this is done is through prayer—the ability of mankind to rule rightly and to rule well through communicating with the invisible God. Man was to look to Him for how he would rule on earth, which is why God instituted communication with Himself.

Our Duties to Rule Earth

Keep in mind that while God has delegated the managerial responsibility for ruling, He has not turned over absolute ownership of the earth to mankind. Yet by delegating the management of the earth to man, God has established a process, within certain boundaries, whereby He respects man's decisions—even if those decisions go against Him, or even if those decisions are not in the best interest of that which is being managed.

While God retains absolute, sovereign authority and ownership, He has delegated relative authority to humanity within the sphere of influence that each person has been placed. For example, the bank may own the house that you live in, but it is your responsibility to pay a monthly mortgage on the house that you say that you "own," as well as to maintain it, for good or for bad. Yes, it feels great to walk into a brand new house that you have just purchased, and think to yourself, *I own this house.* But the truth is, in most cases, the bank owns that house.

The bank does not get involved with the everyday duties of running your house—that is your responsibility—but the bank owns the house. Nor does the bank force you to have a clean house, or prevent you from having a junky one. That is up to you. Yet the bank does not give up ultimate ownership of the house just because you are the one living in it and managing it. If you do not make your payments, you will be the one who faces the consequence of no longer having that house.

The same holds true in the realm where you have been assigned to rule. God is the ultimate owner. He has delegated the responsibility to manage it without having delegated His sovereignty over and within it. Your decisions directly affect the quality of life within the sphere in which you function and will have a large bearing on whether or not your realm of influence increases or decreases with time.

You and I were created and placed on earth to "rule" it, meaning to rule the spheres of influence where we live. That may include our family, community, church, workplace—any number of places. Yet the great tragedy is that so few of us even realize that, and likewise so few recognize the significant and strategic role prayer plays in fulfilling this dominion mandate.

Satan does not want you or I to know our spiritual authority and how to access that authority through prayer because if we knew it, we might just use it to defeat his schemes. This is why he got Adam and Eve to cease communicating with God and start communicating with him so that they would lose access to heavenly authority and wisdom.

> *Kingdom prayer is designed to advance God's kingdom agenda: the visible manifestation of God's rule over all of life.*

The devil never cares much about people going to church, reading their Bibles, or saying cute Christian prayers as long as he and his demons are not exposed to the authoritative nature of our relationship with God. It's the authority that produces power.

But you have been created to oversee the domain in which you function on behalf of God. Through this connection, you possess far more power than you probably even realize. God intentionally created man in His own image in order to act on His behalf in the visible realm, thus reflecting His will in the invisible realm.

Therefore God created us like Him so that we could communicate with Him in order to exercise His will for Him as we reflect Him on earth. This is the goal, nature, and purpose of kingdom prayer. Kingdom prayer is designed to advance God's kingdom agenda, which is the visible manifestation of the comprehensive rule of God over every area of life. When you come to realize all that is actually going on during prayer, it will invigorate your prayer life.

For many of us, prayer can seem boring. If we could only truly grasp all that is happening in the invisible realm in response to our prayers, prayer would be the priority in all of our lives. It would become our first resort and our greatest tool. We would do as Paul says, without needing to be reminded—pray always (1 Thess. 5:16) and pray everywhere (1 Tim. 2:8).

CHAPTER 3

Ruling and Relationship

They line the aisles near the checkout counters where we shop for groceries. They make easy gifts when you are running behind and need to pick up something the last minute for a birthday or holiday party. They are a nice surprise when someone hands you one or you get an email with a code to one inside. They are prepaid gift cards.

Gift cards have become the new craze for giving gifts. In our independent, autonomous society, why not let the receiver choose what he or she wants at a retailer. Plus it saves the buyer time on having to go pick something out.

Gift cards are great . . . kind of. They are great if you use them. But would you believe that approximately one billion dollars worth of gift cards went unused in one year alone? Yes, that's a "b" for billion.[1] I'm as shocked as you are. A billion dollars worth of gift cards were purchased in one year alone that recipients never redeemed.

Thousands of God's Promises

Yet I wonder how God must feel knowing that often we claim none of His many promises found in His Word and ignore how easily accessible He has made Himself through the blood of Christ. We ask for nothing. We seek nothing in His Word, or nothing specific.

"For no matter how many promises God has made, they are 'Yes' in Christ. And so through Him the 'Amen' is spoken by us to the glory of God" (2 Cor. 1:20 NIV). All of the promises of God are yes in Christ. The last I checked there were thousands of these precious promises. Yet how many do you even know? How many do I even know offhand? I think I can answer for most of us: not nearly enough.

While God has given us access to His throne room through prayer and the power of His divine authority as it relates to His promises, we do still have to enter in and get them. No one forced the gift card recipients to cash in their cards. That's why one billion dollars of those cards went unused. Yet something of much greater worth goes unused when we consider what God is willing to do for His children and what they actually call on Him to do.

When prayer is predicated on what God has already declared He will do, you can be assured of His answers. Yet in order to pray this way we need to study His Word (Gk. *logos*), and become intimate with His utterance (*rhema*) so that when we pray, we are praying in line with His will. Scripture states that God has secrets He is willing to share with you and me. We read, "The secret of the Lord is for those who fear Him, and He will make them know His covenant" (Ps. 25:14). God wants you to be so close to Him that He can lean over and whisper His secrets in your ear. When He does or when you discover His promises in His Word, you are then able to take Scripture and pray it right back to Him saying, "God, you said in your Word . . ."

Powerful kingdom prayer involves holding God accountable to what He has already said He would do. God has given us permission in prayer to hold Him to His Word. That means we need to find out what God has said. The foundation of kingdom prayer is knowing what God has already said.

THE SCRIPTURES
AND THE SPIRITUAL BATTLE

We do ourselves a disservice in our prayer lives when we don't take the time to learn and know God's Word. Our prayers become vague, empty words, or they become so full of things God never intended to do. Either way we end up spinning our wheels to no avail. Then we complain, "Hey, I tried and it didn't work!" Often that leads us to call a friend or family member and start laying out our issues on them. Instead we need heaven to invade earth on our behalf. Only heaven holds the answers and the authority to address whatever it is we are lacking or facing in our lives.

Whatever is plaguing you today in the physical realm emanates from the spiritual realm. That is a critical truth to grasp. If you and I do not address the spiritual cause or wage our war in the spiritual realm, we will never get to the cure. This is because everything in the physical is preceded by something in the spiritual. If you want to address something in the physical, you must first address the spiritual cause. Satan wants you to forget that. He doesn't want you to understand the power and authority you have in prayer. He wants you to continue to believe that the problem is your spouse, or your boss, or your friend, or that drink, or that drug, or that emotion—or even you *yourself.* But none of them is the root cause. All are manifestations of the problem—a spiritual battle.

The battle began and continues in the spiritual realm. Thus if you do not address the physical manifestations or lack of manifestations *spiritually*, you will continue to experience the resulting effects of the physical realm's domination.

> God has given us two options. We can leave Him out. Or we can access His wisdom as Ruler over all.

As I mentioned before, when God created the heavens and the earth and placed mankind on it, He said, "Let them rule." God chose to delegate managerial rulership over the earth to mankind. In doing so, He has given us two options. We can leave Him out. The first chapter of the book of Romans summarizes the results of what happens when God is left out. But He also has given us the option to call on Him to access His ultimate authority and wisdom as Ruler over all.

When you go to God and ask for His divine intervention based on His Word, His promises, and His character, then He intervenes in response to your faith and submission to Him, as you acknowledge your need of Him.

You can leave God out. He's given you that option. But you can also bring Him into your plans and actions, primarily through aligning your thoughts with His and then approaching Him through prayer, then watch Him show up in ways you've never even imagined.

DANIEL AND THE ANGELS

A Message from Gabriel

The prophet Daniel is one of the greatest examples of engaging heaven on behalf of earth, and how truly critical it is. One day Daniel is studying God's Word and then responds to Him in prayer based on it. We read,

> In the first year of his reign, I, Daniel, observed in the books the number of the years which was revealed as the word of the Lord to Jeremiah the prophet for the completion of the desolations of Jerusalem, namely, seventy years. So I gave my attention to the Lord God to seek Him by prayer and supplications, with fasting, sackcloth and ashes. (Daniel 9:2–3)

First, Daniel read what God had said to the prophet Jeremiah. Then he prayed on that matter. Daniel continues:

> Now while I was speaking and praying, and confessing my sin and the sin of my people Israel, and presenting my supplication before the Lord my God in behalf of the holy mountain of my God, while I was still speaking in prayer, then the man Gabriel, whom I had seen in the vision previously, came to me in my extreme weariness about the time of the evening offering. He gave me instruction and talked with me and said, "O Daniel, I have now come forth to give you insight with understanding." (Daniel 9:20–22)

God had sent an angel to help Daniel understand even more than he previously had known. However, God did not send the angel to give Daniel understanding *until* he prayed in response to what God had already said. And so Gabriel explains, "At the beginning of your supplications the command was issued, and I have come to tell you, for you are highly esteemed; so give heed to the message and gain understanding of the vision" (v. 23).

Humbled before this mighty angel, Daniel falls to his knees. Gabriel tells him to stand, and then gives the prophet greater insight into his coming:

> "Do not be afraid, Daniel, for from the first day that you set your heart on understanding this and on humbling yourself before your God, your words were heard, and I have come in response to your words. But the prince of the kingdom of Persia was withstanding me for twenty-one days; then behold, Michael, one of the chief princes, came to help me, for I had been left there with the kings of Persia. Now I have come to give you an understanding of what will happen to your people in the latter days, for the vision pertains to the days yet future." When he had spoken to me according to these words, I turned my face toward the ground and became speechless. (10:12–15)

After Daniel had prayed in response to God's words revealed through Jeremiah, God sent an angel to help Daniel. Twice we read in these two chapters that God sent the angel on the exact day that Daniel prayed to God with regard to God's already revealed word. God acted at that very moment in human time. But Daniel had to wait for God's response due to spiritual warfare in the heavenly realm. Gabriel had been dispatched to go to Daniel with a message of understanding from God, but the prince of Persia—a demon—blocked Gabriel from reaching his destination for three weeks ("twenty-one days").

A BATTLE IN THE SPIRITUAL REALM

Don't miss the truth of this and how it may apply to your own life.

The battles you are facing on earth are being waged in the spiritual realm by real beings called angels and demons. When there is a delay in response to your prayer, don't make the assumption that God simply does not care or that He has not heard. Make the assumption, based on His Word, that there is a battle taking place between good and evil. And your prayers can make all the difference in the world as to how quickly that battle plays out.

God not only heard Daniel's prayer when he first offered it, but He also responded immediately to Daniel's prayer. Yet there was a delay in God's response reaching earth. In fact, another angel named Michael was needed to eventually remove the demon from acting as an obstacle for Gabriel. Ultimately, the prince of Persia got double-teamed in order for God to deliver His message to Daniel.

No battle or war has ever lasted a minute. Yet sometimes it seems that is what we believe as Christians because we will say our prayer and then let it go when God doesn't respond immediately. But there are more reasons to keep praying than simply to ask again for the thing that you are seeking. After you ask God, the remainder of your prayers should be focused on thanking God for His promised response. And since there are demons attempting to block the delivery of that answer in your life, your prayers should also focus on asking God to intervene in the situation by removing Satan in case the prince of darkness may be causing a delay in that response.

You need to be on the alert in your prayers because prayers done in response to God's Word are a threat to Satan (1 Peter 5:8; Eph. 5:8). Hell wants to block heaven from reaching earth, and Satan will do anything he can to stop you from praying consistently.

Have you ever noticed that sometimes when you pray, a number of distractions show up? Or you get sleepy when you weren't sleepy before you began? Satan and his demons will try everything they can to stop you from praying because prayer is the vehicle through which God manifests your victory on earth. If we could only truly grasp all that is happening in the invisible realm in response to our prayers, prayer would have the priority on how we spend our time as it ought to be.

Paul emphasizes the spiritual reality in which we live and wage our battles in Ephesians 3 where he explains,

> To me, the very least of all saints, this grace was given, to preach to the Gentiles the unfathomable riches of Christ, and to bring to light what is the administration of the mystery which for ages has been hidden in God who created all things; so that the manifold wisdom of God might now be made known through the church to the rulers and the authorities in the heavenly places. This was in accordance with the eternal purpose which He carried out in Christ Jesus our Lord, in whom we have boldness and confident access through faith in Him. (vv. 8–12)

Paul explains that God, who created all things, wants to make known His mighty wisdom and purpose through His people. His rule and authority over all, including everything in the heavenly places, also is shown through His people. Because God rules and overrules, you and I ought to be ruling the worlds in which we function as well. With the bold "and confident access" (Eph. 3:12) we have been granted, you and I are able and should enter the throne room of God and lay claim to our legal rights, thus overruling any other rule that seeks to defeat us, namely Satan and his heavenly and earthly minions.

This access through prayer is uniquely designed to affect and manifest God's will in history. Prayer is the mechanism to address the battles being waged in the heavenly places that directly affect our physical lives and five senses on earth.

Just as Daniel had to continue to pray in order to dispatch Michael to assist Gabriel in the mission, we must not delay the purposes and plans of God by ceasing to engage in this activity called prayer. Kingdom prayer is so powerful, that those who pray have been able to change God's mind. Consider the prayers of Moses, Hezekiah, and Amos:

> So the Lord *changed His mind* about the harm He said He would do to His people (Ex. 32:14, all emphases added).

> Did Hezekiah king of Judah and all Judah put him to death? Did he not fear the Lord and entreat the favor of the Lord, and the Lord *changed His mind* about the misfortune which He had pronounced against them? (Jer. 26:19).

> I said, "Lord, please pardon! How can Jacob stand, for he is small? The Lord *changed His mind* about this. "It shall not be," said the Lord (Amos 7:2–3).

Scripture records similar times that God said He would do one thing but after the people humbly prayed, God reversed His decision (e.g., Jonah 2:6–10). So when we talk about this thing called kingdom prayer, we are not talking about a minor thing. God says that this access of prayer actually reaches up into the heavenly realm and pulls down to earth God's purposes. Or as the Lord's prayer so eloquently states, "Thy kingdom come, Thy will be done."

But God is not going to act arbitrarily. He has created processes to work with this go-between called prayer connecting the two realms together. That is why Scripture says, "You do not have because you do not ask" (James 4:2). It is not saying you do not have because God is not able, or God is not willing, but simply because you have not taken part in the process of prayer. You have not asked. Kingdom prayer is calling forth in history what God has determined from eternity. It is bringing into the physical what God has predetermined in the spiritual.

Relationship is Foundational

Don't confuse that last statement with assuming you can call into being anything you want. The secret to answered prayer is alignment with God. It is being in such unison with God that you are praying according to His will. Once, when one of the disciples asked Jesus to show them the Father, Christ responded with a powerful treatise on prayer. He said,

> "Do you not believe that I am in the Father, and the Father is in Me? The words that I say to you I do not speak on My own initiative, but the Father abiding in Me does His works. Believe Me that I am in the Father and the Father is in Me; otherwise believe because of the works themselves. Truly, truly, I say to you, he who believes in Me, the works that I do, he will do also; and greater works than these he will do; because I go to the Father. Whatever you ask in My name, that will I do, so that the Father may be glorified in the Son. If you ask Me anything in My name, I will do it." (John 14:10–14)

Like a parent to a child, Jesus attempted to walk the disciples through the logical flow of understanding the answer to their question. Bottom line: You have seen the Father because His works have been done through Me. In other words, we are close and that's why My prayers get answered.

Jesus then took it a step further to teach His followers, and us, that we have access to that same capacity to do even greater works than what Jesus did while on earth. We access this capacity when we align ourselves with Jesus, who is aligned with the Father, and receive the wisdom needed to ask according to God's will and in Christ's name. When we reach a level of intimacy with God similar to what Christ experienced while on earth, we will exercise authority in our prayers—the likes of which are rarely seen these days.

You know how you can get so close to somebody—a friend or loved one, or even a coworker—that you can finish their sentences for them simply because you have been hanging in their presence for so long? You can predict where their train of thought is headed, read their expressions, and tap into their mood. That's relational intimacy. Jesus says when we reach this level of intimacy with God, we will pray in alignment with His will.

> *The secret to answered prayer is alignment with God. It is praying according to His will.*

That's power. But that power comes with effort. It comes with seeking the Lord, spending time with Him, setting aside your own selfish desires, and humbling yourself before God and with others. Power in prayer is free. Jesus paid the price for our access to God's throne. But power in prayer does not come without passionately pursuing the Lord with all your heart, all your mind, all your strength, and all your soul. It comes through linking up with the Lord relationally while surrendering to Him spiritually.

Sometimes we confuse prayer with being an action more so than it is an abiding. Abide in Christ, be intimate with God—and powerful prayer can be as simple as holding up two loaves and five fish and thanking God for feeding thousands.

CHAPTER 4

Precision and Persistence

Most cars now include cruise control. We press a button, the car takes over, and we just roll along at a consistent speed. Barring something happening that forces us to hit the brakes, we're often satisfied to cruise. While that way of navigating may be fine for a car, it's an unacceptable form of Christian living.

If your spiritual life is on cruise control, it means you've taken your foot off of the accelerator. I can assure you that a cruise-control Christian will never experience the level of God's reality that He has intended for them.

We start our week on Sunday when we come to church, and then as we leave the parking lot we turn on a spiritual cruise control. We just let the Christian life roll on until we turn the ignition off the following Sunday morning, come to church . . . and then we reset cruise for another week.

You may be on cruise control *right now*. My goal in looking at this subject of kingdom prayer in the Scriptures is to encourage you to hit the brakes: to take your life out of cruise control. By the end of this book, I hope you will begin to allow God to actively lead you in the various dimensions of your life through this intimate and authoritative process called prayer.

In 1 Chronicles 14:2, we read, "David realized that the Lord had established him as king over Israel, and that his kingdom was highly exalted, for the sake of His people Israel." David has been royally blessed. God has taken a shepherd boy and raised him to a position of prominence. It was during this time of blessing that David runs into a problem. We read in verse 8: "When the Philistines heard that David had been anointed king over all Israel, all the Philistines went up in search of David; and David heard of it and went out against them."

Isn't that just how life works sometimes? As soon as you've been blessed, something seems to go wrong. You are praising God for what He did in the morning, and by the afternoon you are dealing with the Philistines. David realized God had raised him up but then he turns around to discover the enemy is coming after him.

Here's where things really get interesting. The enemy has come to mess things up for David in the middle of his blessing. We know that David's first reaction is to go to war against them. But suddenly David remembers he has not yet prayed. He is doing things on his own.

TIME TO STOP . . . AND PRAY

David recognizes he's going solo and he takes action. He doesn't just cruise along. He asks God a question: "Shall I go against the Philistines? And will You give them into my hand?" Then the Lord said to him, "Go up, for I will give them into your hand" (v. 10).

Now, this wasn't David's first rodeo. He'd been to battle before. He had even experienced success in battle, so he could have easily just determined to use an older strategy or approach to this situation. But he doesn't. Rather, David comes to the Lord and he starts with a question. He says, "Shall I go up against the Philistines?" It's a strange question because we saw in the previous verse that David is already on his way to face his enemies.

But he asks, "God, should I keep doing this? I *plan* to do it. I *think* I should do it. I think I can do it, but is what I'm doing what You want done? Shall I go up against them?"

David does two important things. First, he asks a specific question. Second, he recognizes he has already begun to take action before praying for guidance, so he interrupts what he is doing to ask a precise prayer looking for a precise answer. *Do I keep going, God—or do You have another plan?*

Pray Specifically and Pray Early

The simple reason that so many of our prayers hit the ceiling is because our prayers can become so general that they don't say much of anything at all.

"God, give me guidance."

"Lord, bless my day."

"Lord, cover my family."

"Father, help me on my job."

"God, give me strength and good health."

"How about a mate?" Or if your marriage is shaky, "Please fix this marriage."

Any of those sound familiar? Too often we toss up general prayers when the answer we need isn't general at all. We need a precise answer, but we do not bother to pause what we are doing and ask a specific prayer.

Another reason we don't see more of God is He doesn't get

> *God deserves to be first. Kingdom prayer respects the King enough to come to Him first.*

invited in on the front end. We want to bring heaven in after we've hit the snag or run into the issue. But God wants us to inquire of Him before we open our mouth to say anything to anyone else. That's why there's so much in the Bible about the word *first*. Love the Lord thy God *first* (Matt. 22:37) that Jesus might "have *first place* in everything" (Col. 1:18, emphasis added). Give God the *first* fruits (Prov. 3:9). God does not want to be on the tail end of your life.

He is God, after all. He deserves to be first. You are finite, meaning you are limited. God is infinite. Infinite means He's unlimited. You know what is and you can look back to what was. God knows what was, what is, what will be, and what could have been. Kingdom prayer respects the King enough to come to Him first.

God is the only One who can answer the question "What if?" God is the only One who knows the best course of action for you to take. Or the best words for you to say in the conversation you are about to have. Or the best use of your time—the list goes on and on. David inquired of God because he believed God had more information than he did. David prayed because he understood the value of communicating with God. When he did, he got God's reply, "Go up, for I will give them into your hand" (1 Chron. 14:10). Not only did God tell David what to do—He told him what the result would be as well.

When you get information like that you can move forward

with assurance. You are not guessing anymore. This is why, in the New Testament, Jesus didn't make a move without checking with His Father first. Now, if the Son of God—*who is God*—had to check with His Father before He made a move, how much more do you and I, who are not even remotely close to being God, need to check with God before we make a move?

David inquired of God for a specific answer to a specific need. Most of us, for one reason or another, don't do that. We pray general prayers but we fail to invite God to move in specific moments. Thus, many of our specific moments go wasted or wind up in a mess.

Significantly, when a similar situation occurs, King David again prays for guidance. We read:

> The Philistines made yet another raid in the valley. David inquired again of God, and God said to him, "You shall not go up after them; circle around behind them and come at them in front of the balsam trees. It shall be when you hear the sound of marching in the tops of the balsam trees, then you shall go out to battle, for God will have gone out before you to strike the army of the Philistines." David did just as God had commanded him. (vv. 13–16)

This time God gave an entirely different response to a very similar question. Once again David prepares to fight the Philistines. The previous time, the Lord told him to go up and face them. But this time, the Lord gives different instructions. The point is that when God gives us a clear answer to prayer, or a clear guidance and direction, we should not assume it applies to every situation. God is flexible, and His methods change. Follow David's model and inquire of God in every situation. Had David assumed the first direction was good for the second battle, his troops would have been annihilated.

Now, you may be thinking: *Well, David's story is in the Old Testament, when God talked to people. They could clearly hear God's voice.* While it's true that in the Old Testament God did sometimes verbally communicate with His people, He continues to speak to us today. He does this through His Word and through His Holy Spirit (see John 14:26; 16:13; 1 Cor. 2:9–13). No matter how God chooses to talk to us, we need to hold firm to the truth that if we seek Him, we will find Him. If we call on Him, we will hear Him.

The lesson to learn from David and his battle is that we are to seek God in prayer before we move forward. Look at prayer in the same way you look at a GPS *before* you start driving. Prayer is a tool to access God on the front end of the situations of your life. Just as you would turn on your GPS before you got lost, make it a habit to seek God's precise direction first before you set out on a discussion or a decision. Like David, you will find things flow much more smoothly that way and you will receive the answers to your prayers more specifically and more completely.

PRAY WITH PERSISTENCE

Praying with precision is a critical component to answered prayer. But praying with persistence also comes into play. Struggles have a way of heightening the intentionality of our prayers. Yet when we see no improvement over time, it is easy to think that our prayers aren't making any difference and to stop, or give up.

However, Jesus does not want us to stop praying. To show us how important persistence is, He taught this principle through a parable, the story of a persistent woman (Luke 18:1–6).

The Persistent Woman

In a particular city lives a judge who fears neither God nor man. He cares not what anyone else thinks or says about him but rather rests in his position as judge. This judge heard numerous cases. He could be compared to what we had in early American history as a circuit judge, someone who traveled from town to town to try cases and settle disputes. Over time, this judge had gained a reputation as an "unrighteous judge" (v. 6). Judges like this one were easy targets for bribes paid by the wealthy in return for favorable rulings.

The woman in our story is not wealthy. As a widow she most likely has little money or influence. Seeing as she represents herself reveals to us that she has no one to defend her. She cannot afford legal representation, and no one in her family apparently has come forward to help. She doesn't stand a chance at getting a just verdict in her case, yet regardless of the impossibility of justice, she does not give up. She presses on, alone and on her own.

Jesus didn't give us the specifics of her case—like what the charges are or how she has been wronged. That isn't the important part. What is important is how she faced it. When faced with someone who was out to do her wrong and without the ability, money, or power to stop them, she has turned to the law.

Yet the story tells us clearly that the judge just does not care that she has been wronged and is seeking his assistance. He is not moved by her plight and it does not matter to him that this woman is entitled to legal rights.

What Jesus points out through this story is that even though the judge did not possess a heart to help the woman, he did intervene on her behalf simply due to her persistence. As Jesus explains, "For a while he was unwilling; but afterward he said to himself,

'Even though I do not fear God nor respect man, yet because this widow bothers me, I will give her legal protection, otherwise by continually coming she will wear me out'" (Luke 18:4–5).

The Weary Judge

The judge had had it. This woman had continually brought her problem to him, time and time again. This didn't make him care about her issue any more than at the start. But he did care about himself and his own peace of mind. Because of that, he gave her what she asked for. He gave her the legal protection that was her right to have.

We know how strongly this unjust judge felt about the tenacity of this woman because the Greek word that is translated into "wear me out" literally means to "give a black eye." To give a black eye meant to ruin his reputation. Not only was the woman wearing out the unjust judge mentally, but he knew that if she kept coming she had the potential to ruin his name because of his refusal to fulfill his legal obligation as a judge. The law was on her side. Evidently, this woman was showing up in a public court, telling the judge he was failing to do what was right. She had taken it as a matter reflecting the ability of the judge. She questioned his name, and she did it publicly.

Persistent prayer makes it a kingdom issue. God cares about His righteous reputation.

Jesus makes an interesting contrast between the widow and the unjust judge and us before God Himself. "Now, will not God bring about justice for His elect who cry to Him day and night, and will He delay long over them? I tell you that He will bring about justice for them quickly" (vv. 7–8). Jesus tells us plainly that if an unjust judge who cares not for righteousness or even the person bringing the claim will respond to a woman because of her persistence, how much more will God—who is just, righteous, and compassionate—grant us our legal rights bound to us through Him and His covenant?

The widow was a stranger to the judge. We are not strangers to God. We (the elect) are God's chosen ones—we are His children. You and I who belong to Jesus Christ make up His elect. If an unrighteous judge will grant legal protection to a stranger in order to protect his own reputation, how much more will God bring about justice to His own children not only for the sake of His own name but for the sake of those whom He loves? Jesus makes it clear: He will not delay in doing so when you seek Him as the woman sought out the judge.

Persistent prayer based on God's law makes it a kingdom issue, and God cares about His righteous reputation. However, far too many of us look at the impossibility before us rather than the power to Whom we speak. So we simply give up too soon or fail to attach our request to God's Word.

Appealing to Righteous Authority

Jesus includes an interesting phrase in this parable. In fact, it shows up twice. The phrase is "legal protection" (vv. 3, 5). The issue at hand was not whether the judge knew the woman, liked the woman, or even felt sorry for the woman; the issue on the table was the law. She was seeking what was rightfully and legally hers.

If you are a citizen of the United States of America, you have certain rights and privileges that come with your citizenship. Because you belong to this country, there are constitutional rights of which you can appeal to the courts if they are violated. Of course it is also possible to be a citizen of the United States and have rights that either you are unaware of or of which you do not take full advantage. Just because you are a US citizen does not automatically mean you are benefiting fully from your birthright. Awareness and access must both be used to take advantage of the kingdom authority that is yours.

Similarly, as believers of Christ and children of the King, we are citizens of heaven. Each of us born again into the family of God is entitled to the rights and privileges that come from that birthright available through the cross. Yet just as being ignorant of your rights and privileges as a citizen of America can potentially keep you from them, the same is true regarding what is yours as a citizen of the heavenly kingdom. As a citizen of heaven, you have been granted access to heaven for help on earth, in history. This is a covenantal right secured by blood for those in the kingdom of God (Heb. 4:16).

Be aware that the issues you may be facing or struggling with in your life or in your prayers may be issues of the covenantal rights you have. If they are, you are free to appeal to God based on your legal position and rights. You are free to hold Him accountable to His own precepts and truth. And you are free to persistently remind Him through prayer of what is rightfully yours under His rule. Even though the unjust judge did not care for the woman, he responded to her request and gave her what was legally hers because she kept confronting him with the law.

God is a God of covenant. He is also a God of His Word. He has obligated Himself to His own Word. He has tied His name and His reputation to what He Himself has said. He is tethered to His own covenantal agreements. And because God is by nature righteous, He is committed to His own righteous standard and will operate in concert with His own covenant.

The problems arise in our prayer lives when too few of us truly understand what our spiritual rights are. Had the widow not known what she was entitled to by law, she would have nothing to come to the unjust judge about. Yet because she knew the law, and knew what the judge was legally obligated to give her, she was able to confidently come again and again to ask for what was legally hers to have. It was her knowledge of the law that gave her a basis on which to stand.

Your knowledge of God's promises and His precepts will give you a basis on which to stand in your prayers. Because the widow knew the law, and kept appealing to the judge based on the law, she received what was duly hers. If an unjust judge will submit to the law even though he does not have regard for it, think how much more a holy and righteous God will grant you what is rightfully yours as His child when you ask Him for it. God is bound to His Word and that gives you kingdom authority in prayer.

You need to pray according to the promises of God. When you know your rights based on His truth, you can call on God with the authority to get what you deserve based on your legal status granted through the blood of Jesus Christ and the new covenant. The best way to pray is to hold God to His own Word.

Open your Bible and pray, "God, let me show You what You said because You don't lie [see Titus 1:2 NIV]. This is what You said, and this is what I'm asking for in Jesus' name." Those kinds of prayers, based on God's Word, get answers. They get answers quickly as Jesus said, "I tell you that He will bring about justice for them quickly" (Luke 18:8). When He is ready to move, He will move fast.

In terms of what He has written, God is committed first and foremost to His Word—to His covenant. God is not bound to what you think. He is not bound to what others think. He's not even bound to what you feel.

But He is bound to His Word.

If and when you learn how to pray in alignment with His Word, you will witness the supernatural on a whole new level. You will see the King intervene on behalf of His rule, His authority, and in response to your informed, persistent prayers.

CHAPTER 5

Accessing the Able

As a boy growing up in Baltimore, my neighborhood swimming pool appeared on any hot Saturday night when the fire marshall would come and open the hydrant. We'd put on our shorts and all the kids in the neighborhood would run outside after the marshall left and we would have fun playing in the water gushing from the hydrant.

But one thing always confused me about this mysterious red hydrant, so one day I asked my dad. "How can this pipe hold all this water?" The water would be gushing out for hours and I couldn't figure out how one three-foot pipe could contain so much water.

My dad quickly set me straight. "Son, that pipe has no water in it at all. The water is in the reservoir—Druid Hill Reservoir. All the fire hydrant does is deliver the water here from there." He then explained that the reservoir never ran out because when it rained, the reservoir would fill back up. That way the fire department had access to enough water whenever they needed it through an underground pipe system connecting the hydrant to the reservoir.

The unseen connection that delivered water was the large underground pipes. That small hydrant was able to provide a powerful delivery because it was ultimately connected to a huge source. My father told me, "If there is no connection, there is no water."

To paraphrase my dad's words, if there is no abiding connection with God through prayer, there is no access to the vast resources of God's kingdom authority and power. God is the reservoir and He is able to supply all that you need, but there has to be a connection beneath the surface, in your soul and spirit. Otherwise, when you go to access that which you need, you will find nothing there. Remember, it's not the hydrant that supplies the water—it's the reservoir. And the connection that supplies the force is our infinite God.

GOD IS ABLE—BUT ARE WE CONNECTED?

God *is* able, but you must be connected to God to tap into His power. And the apostle Paul describes that abundant power as he continued in Ephesians 3: "Now to Him who is able to do far more abundantly beyond all we can ask or think, according to the power that works in us" (v. 20).

You have probably heard this verse before. We all love to say that God is able, especially when we need Him to do something. But let's take a closer look at this passage, because in its construct lies some important truths.

"Now to Him" points us upward to God. It focuses our gaze on God because He is the Source of all that is able. Next, Paul explains that God "is able to do far more abundantly beyond all we can ask or think." That's the best news we can receive, especially when we are losing heart. God *is* able.

Daniel Connected by Prayer

Those words got me thinking about what in particular God is able to do, so I looked up some places in Scripture where it uses this phrase "He is able." First I found the story of Shadrach, Meshach, and Abednego in Daniel 3. These young men had a problem. King Nebuchadnezzar had ordered everyone to bow down to an image he set up to show allegiance to him or be thrown into a fiery furnace. These three young Jewish men refused because God was their one true God and they could not bow before the huge idol.

Nebuchadnezzar was mad. He asked, "And what god is there who can deliver you out of my hand?" And the three young men answered the king in confidence: "Our God whom we serve is able to deliver us from the furnace of blazing fire" (3:15, 17).

Shadrach, Meshach, and Abednego knew that Nebuchadnezzar had the furnace. They knew he had the match. But they also knew something that King Nebuchadnezzar didn't—their God *was able* to deliver them through the fiery circumstances of life, those circumstances that wanted to consume them. And God did.

And let's take a quick look at Daniel. A law was passed that decreed that the people could not pray to any other god but the god of the Medes and Persians for thirty days (Daniel 6). When Daniel heard this, he went home, opened his windows, got down on his knees, and prayed to the God of heaven.

Now most of us—if we were brave enough to go against this decree in the first place—would have probably snuck home, closed the window so no one could see us, and prayed standing up. But that wasn't Daniel's pattern. Instead, he didn't change his habit. He prayed with his windows open and faced Jerusalem, where God's temple was located. He prayed boldly on his knees (Dan. 6:10), and eventually "several men came by agreement and found Daniel making petition before his God" (v. 11). They reported the activity to the king and urged him to enforce his decree—that required any violator be thrown into the lions' den. And that is exactly what King Darius did. But the next morning, the king came to the pit and shouted down to Daniel, "Has your God . . . been able to deliver you from the lions?" (v. 20). And there was Daniel, praising God, alive and totally unscratched. God is able.

Two Blind Men Connected by Faith in Jesus

Don't misunderstand. God doesn't always deliver you *from*. Sometimes He delivers you *through*, and sometimes He delivers you *in*. But I can testify that *God is able*. In Matthew 9, two blind men come to Jesus, God incarnate who came to earth, and ask Jesus to help them see. The Lord asked a question in return. "Do you believe I am able?" (v. 28).

Jesus wanted to know if they thought He could do it.

Are We Connected by Faith?

Sometimes that is a question Jesus wants to know of us as well. Friend, do you believe that Jesus is able? Able to find solutions for your health even when the doctors have no answers? Solutions to your marriage when it looks hopeless? Solutions to your career, finances or even your emotions? Jesus *is* able.

Hebrews 7:25 tells us that Jesus "is able to save completely" (NIV). He is able to take those who you don't think *could* be saved and bring them into His family of saints. Jesus is able.

Second Corinthians 9:8 says that "God is able to make all

grace abound to you so that . . . in everything you might have an abundance." God is able to meet your every need. And not only that, He will meet your every need *abundantly*.

> *The people of God will take action because they know that God is able.*

Jude 25 tells us that "[God] is able to keep you from stumbling." He is able to sustain you. Daniel declared, "And the people who know their God will display strength and take action" (11:32). The people of God will *handle* any situation at hand, but not passively. They will *act*. They will *move*. They will *take action* because they know their God and therefore they have *power*. Why? Because they know that *God is able!*

MAKING THE CONNECTION BY PRAYER

But let's look again at Ephesians 3:20–21: "Now to Him who is able to do far more abundantly beyond all that we ask or think, according to the power that works within us, to Him be the glory in the church and in Christ Jesus to all generations forever and ever."

Jesus is able to do far and beyond what you can ask or even think of. He comes through in ways you didn't expect. Ways that will blow your mind and make you say, "Where did that come from? How did that happen?" And ways that make it impossible for you to take the credit. When you're losing heart, you're not looking for ordinary. When you're losing heart, you're looking for extraordinary. God addresses the losing-heart situation with power. He wants you to know that He *is* able.

But there's a condition—a condition we often overlook. The

condition is God acts "according to the power that works in us" (v. 20b). That has to do with our connection to God through prayer and His Spirit.

Yes, God *is* able. Yes, God can do "far more abundantly beyond all we ask" or imagine. Yes, God can provide more than you could even think possible—just like the short fire hydrant that is able to pour out a continuous flow of water despite how it looks. But also just like the hydrant, unless you are connected with God through relational communion and communication with Him through kingdom prayer, Him being "able" will do you little to no good.

You have to connect with Christ as He dwells within you to access what He is able to do. God looks at the power within before He determines the action without. If there is no kingdom power within because Jesus Christ is not at home in you so you are not being filled to the full, there will be no kingdom power coming out. God will not be free to express Himself at the level of His capacity because the power within determines the power without.

You must open every room of your life for Him to flow through you. If Jesus hasn't been invited into every aspect of your life, you will miss out on His power in your life and in your prayers. It's the intimacy that determines the capacity.

Return with me to Niagara Falls to help illustrate this. As you recall, as a visitor, you don't truly experience the Falls until you get on the boat, the Maid of the Mist, and ride close to it. Now imagine you on that boat holding a thimble you planned to fill with some of this water. If you leaned over the railing and filled up your thimble, you would get a thimbleful of the Niagara River. But that is all you would get. Even though an enormous amount of water is cascading from the top of the Falls, once this thimble is full, everything else spills over the edges onto the boat or back into the river.

Now if you had a glass and stuck it out to catch some water, you would definitely get more than your thimble held. But, again, it's only a glassful. Because once the water hit the top of the glass, it's over. Whatever else that comes pouring into it would just overflow onto the boat and back into the river.

> *Open every room of your life for Him to flow through you.*

What if you brought a big bucket? Yes, you would get more than a thimble and more than the glass, but you still would not get more than the bucket, because once the bucket became full, that's all the Niagara would give you. Not because it couldn't give you more or that it didn't have more, but because you couldn't handle more. Even if you brought a barrel to fill, the outcome would be the same. You would catch much more water, but once that barrel became full, that's all you would get.

Even if you could bring a tanker to the lower Niagara River and fill its large hold with water from the falls, once the tanker was full it could give no more of the Falls. Niagara Falls has a lot to give. So the issue wouldn't be how much it can give. The issue would be how much can you hold.

See, a lot of us want a tanker full of answered prayers when we have a thimbleful of relationship. We are busy praying down blessing after blessing and power after power—we want deliverance, guidance, peace, and all else. But the power of the prayer is tied to the size of the container. It is "according to the power working in you." That's a measurement term. However much power you have working in you is the level of power God is able to work outwardly as well.

Paul instructs us to be filled to all the fullness of God. When we are, we can rise to the level God intends for us.

What abiding prayer does is increase the capacity to access that overflowing power. When you increase that capacity, you will find yourself handling more things at once. You will discover the ability to access a greater level of God's answered prayer. You will experience the flow of His power through you and discover the secret to increased productivity, motivation, and endurance. Rather than "lose heart," you will gain momentum as you allow His power to become your strength.

PART 2

The Context
of Kingdom
Prayer

CHAPTER 6

Faith and Futility

Watch out for Heather Dorniden," she heard the announcer say. *Yeah, watch out for Heather,* she thought as she rounded the corner in the final lap of the race.[1] Three runners loomed far in front of her, too far to catch even with a heroic last kick. Or so most rational people would have thought.

It's not that Heather wasn't an excellent runner to begin with. She was. In fact, in high school she had five times been crowned an All-State performer. Running now on a track scholarship for the University of Minnesota, Heather had been a favorite to claim the title for this 600-meter race at the Big Ten Indoor Championships her junior year in college.

She was slated as the likely winner—until she tripped during her final heat and landed on her face 200 meters from the finish line.

Just one more lap from the finish line, Heather's feet became ensnared with another runner's, sending her sprawling head-first onto the unforgiving track. This wasn't a slight fall, either. Heather skidded so far that she left marks across her stomach. She lay there several seconds.

To Heather, it didn't matter so much that she had fallen down. What mattered more was that she must get back up because her teammates were in a bid to clinch the Big Ten Women's Indoor Track Championship. She got up, she would later recount, because she didn't want to let them down.

Fall or no fall, Heather was going to finish.

Trailing a good thirty meters by the time she got back on her feet, Heather looked up at the three runners far ahead. About midway down the backside of the final lap, she passed the first of the three runners. Wild cheers rose from the stands, fans urging her to do the impossible. Rounding the back corner on the final stretch, Heather then "hit a gear" she didn't even know she had, propelling her past the second runner. With only one more to catch, she continued to close the lead. Near the finish line Heather made a final lunge—and won her heat! The University of Minnesota's track team would go on to win the Big Ten Women's Track Championship after all.

But Heather won much more than that on what could have been a day that destroyed her. Rather than staying down, she dared a comeback that—thanks to YouTube replays—eventually would inspire a world of watchers[2] to realize that despite falling, you can still win.

"It's something that is completely unexplainable to me besides through a higher power," she would later say. "I feel like the Lord just filled me up and gave me the opportunity to show what amazing things can happen through Him."[3]

Amazing things, indeed. Or as Paul would put it, exceedingly abundantly above all you could ask or imagine, "far more abundantly than all that we ask or think" (Eph. 3:20), as we noted in the last chapter. God can do those things everyone else says are impossible.

That is exactly why we pray. We know He *is* able. It's just accessing that "able" that has been known to cause us some of our own stumbles from time to time—just as it did for another woman whose issues far too often brought her to her knees—not because she tripped and had fallen, but in the sheer pain of unanswered prayer.

HANNAH'S PRAYER

The Pain of Her Unanswered Prayer

The Bible tells us that our bodies can become physically sick when we go for too long in a state of hopelessness. "Hope deferred makes the heart sick" (Prov. 13:12). This is how we find Hannah as her story is told to us in 1 Samuel. She was not doing well at all.

Hannah never ran track like Heather, but she showed no less resolve in seeking the goal for which her heart truly longed. Married to a man at a time in biblical culture when multiple wives was accepted, Hannah found herself outpaced and out-raced on the track that mattered most to women at that time—family. Her husband's other wife had already born him children, "but Hannah had no children" (1 Samuel 1:2).

We know that her husband loved her dearly, despite her lack, because we read that he "would give a double portion [of food], for he loved Hannah, but the Lord had closed her womb" (v. 5). Yet even with her husband's love, Hannah knew children secured their future and offered a legacy. Children were an essential part of life, especially as parents aged. Hannah wanted nothing more than to have a child.

Hannah's rival enjoyed witnessing her defeat over and over each year. Peninnah would not be considered a good sport on today's field of play. She was a bully who taunted Hannah regularly. We read, "Her rival, however, would provoke her bitterly to irritate her, because the Lord had closed her womb. It happened year after year, as often as she went up to the house of the Lord, she would provoke her; so she [Hannah] wept and would not eat" (vv. 6–7).

Hannah was in a desperate situation. Not only that, her fall—unlike Heather's—lasted more than moments. It went on for years. There's something about a crisis that is prolonged that drains the hope even more deeply. Prolonged trials can make it even more difficult to pray. It's like sitting in an emergency room and waiting for your name to be called but watching everyone else go in one by one. While you are in pain, confusion and worry, time seems to slow to a crawl. Yet those around you don't even seem to care. If you aren't careful, your feelings will soon dominate your faith.

If a doctor had been able to examine Hannah, he would have chalked it up to something biologically wrong. But as verse 5 reveals, it wasn't Hannah's body that had betrayed her. Rather, the Lord had closed her womb.

Hannah's issue wasn't physical at all. It was spiritual—like so many of the issues we face today. The reason Hannah couldn't conceive was God Himself blocking her conception.

Similarly, many of the problems, emptiness, barrenness, or complications that we face in our own lives aren't as tied to the physical realm as they may appear. That's a reminder that we judge what we are facing not merely by what we can see. Instead we each should ask whether God has something to do with our inability to produce, bear fruit, overcome or achieve. Hannah's physical limitation and her emotional irritation by her rival had a reason, which God would reveal at a later time. The trials and troubles you might be facing right now also have a reason. If you find yourself praying for something for a prolonged period of time—and feel you are getting nowhere—ask God to reveal what He is doing behind the scenes. He may not—but sometimes just understanding that there is a bigger kingdom plan in play can provide you with the patience you need during times of waiting.

Although she received no reply to her prayers, Hannah models for us what we are to do when our prayers remain unanswered for a long time. Her emptiness hadn't stopped her from going to the temple year after year, bowing her head, or seeking the spiritual. She "hung in there," waiting for her change to come.

The Tears of Her Prayers

One day, it looked like it all became too much for Hannah. She broke down in desperation and wept.

Sometimes it is okay to cry. It is okay to reach that point where you admit you cannot go any further, apart from God's intervening hand. Life is hard. Hannah had had more than she could handle, and the Scripture tells us she "wept bitterly" (v. 10).

Hannah's wailing meant she had reached the end of her rope. Hers was a deep pain that knew no comfort.

Weeping bitterly usually comes when we have lost all hope for change. It is in those desperate times that desperate measures—things we normally wouldn't do—come to our mind. For Hannah it was a major decision to surrender the very child she yearned for. She would give her child back to God if He would give him to her at all. So she prayed, "O Lord of hosts, if You will indeed look on the affliction of Your maidservant and remember me, and . . . give Your maidservant a son, then I will give him to the Lord all the days of his life, and a razor shall never come on his head" (v. 11).

The Motive of Her Prayer—and Ours

Hannah had been praying to get pregnant for years. Her desire for a child was so strong that she was willing to let go of the thing she wanted most if she could but have him for a while. That brings us to a very important point regarding prayer. In Hannah's prayer, she let God know what He would gain through answering her. She made it about Him. She focused on how His kingdom would be advanced and His name glorified. That is a heart in alignment under God.

Far too often, we don't even give consideration to how God will benefit when He answers our prayers. We are paying too much attention to what we want that we forget this world and our lives were created for God's purposes. He has a plan. He has a kingdom agenda. If you want your prayers answered or your requests granted, then consider how that answer will benefit God and His kingdom. If it doesn't, then you may have to acknowledge you are asking with selfish motives rather than out of a heart that loves God first (Luke

> *If you want your prayers answered, consider how that answer will benefit God and His kingdom.*

10:27). We are commanded to put God first in our lives and with our lives, and yet frequently we don't even consider Him, His desires, His will in our prayers.

Ask yourself these questions regarding your prayers:

- Is what I'm praying for going to benefit others?
- Does my request, if granted, bring glory to God?
- How will this request advance God's kingdom agenda on earth?
- Will the answer to my prayer equip me to serve God more fully?

These are the types of questions to run your prayer needs through to align your heart's motivation with God's will. Hannah wanted a son, yes. But she knew first and foremost that her life was ultimately about God and His rule. So she made a strategic decision with regard to her prayer need. She aligned it underneath God's hand. She literally chose to give to Him her heart's desire. And, remember, this was no small desire. Hannah longed for a child as much as was humanly possible.

Even her demeanor reflected a woman distressed in grief as she made her vow to the Lord. The priest nearby as Hannah prayed at the temple thought she was drunk (v. 14). Hannah was a mess. Sometimes troubles can get so deep that our eyes—and soul—shed tears. With respect and sincerity she corrected the mistaken priest:

> "No, my lord, I am a woman oppressed in spirit; I have drunk neither wine nor strong drink, but I have poured out my soul before the Lord. Do not consider your maidservant as a worthless woman, for I have spoken until now out of my great concern and provocation." (vv. 15–16)

Lessons from Hannah—and Heather

The priest heard more than Hannah's words; he heard her heart. He believed her, blessed her, and told her that God would give her the child for whom she had asked.

Scripture records that when Hannah heard what the priest had to say, she believed him and went on her way no longer sad (v. 17). She had faith that her prayer—her vow—would be answered.

Hannah Moves Forward in Faith

What happened next is often overlooked in the study of the life of Hannah. Just two verses summarize it but it reveals a lot about the ingredients of faith. And remember, faith leads to answered prayers, so if you are trying to pray with power and authority, one thing to focus on would be your faith. Let's learn from Hannah.

First, Hannah moved forward in faith. For starters, we read that Hannah ate. She had been hurt for so long not only by her own barrenness but also by the taunting of her rival that Hannah had stopped eating for some time. Yet with the news from the priest that her prayer would be answered, Hannah returned to a state of calm that enabled her appetite to come back. She began to feed her body and regain her strength.

Then, in the next verse we discover that Hannah had relations with her husband, sexual intimacy. For couples who have tried to conceive for year after year, the act of intimacy can become a reminder of loss and pain. It can turn from the joyous celebration it was intended to be into a task filled with emptiness and regret. It's beyond "Why bother" to "I don't want to be reminded of what we never get." But Hannah and her husband didn't allow the years of barrenness to change their behavior. Upon word from the priest that she would conceive, Hannah and her husband acted in faith.

One of the mistakes that we often make as we face the various trials and challenges in our lives is that of inactivity. When the mountain seems too high to climb or too large to move, we sit back and leave it all for God to do. But too often God is waiting on us while we think we are waiting on Him. He is waiting to see if we will do our actions of faith, even in the face of the impossible. Had Hannah *not* had relations with her husband, she would never have gotten pregnant.

HEATHER CONTINUED TO RUN

Had Heather Dorniden not gotten up from the track, she would have never won. In fact, she continued to run after college. Later, as she neared her thirties, Heather still raced, and even made the USA national team for the IAFF World Indoor Track and Field Championships.[4] Hers was an unlikely bid but she kept training and eventually made it.

"Relying on the Lord's plan does not imply 'lack of action,'" Heather later wrote on her blog about her surprise late placement on the national team, "but rather an openness for His infinite power, strength, courage, and grace to work through me. I intend to approach these races with confidence and purpose, clothed in the armor of Christ. I will perform to the best of my ability with trust that this is all part of a plan much bigger than me, and I am not alone."[5]

Hannah's pregnancy was much bigger than her. Heather's win was much bigger than her. Your prayers, and the answers to them, are much bigger than you. God has a plan to impact others through you which is why He will often let us get to the point where we know it is He who brought it about. But that will not come about without action tied to your faith.

Faith never implies lack of action. Faith is a participatory sport. It means acting like God is telling the truth. Or as you will hear me say several times: *Faith is acting like something is so even when it is not so in order that it might be so simply because God said so.*

Hannah Gives Up Her Plans for His

Hannah did more than sit around and wait for God to send a stork with her special package. Rather, she acted on the truth that God was going to give her a son. And then, when He did, she fulfilled her vow and gave him back to Him. We read,

> So the woman remained and nursed her son until she weaned him. Now when she had weaned him, she took him up with her, with a three-year-old bull and one ephah of flour and a jug of wine, and brought him to the house of the Lord in Shiloh, although the child was young. Then they slaughtered the bull, and brought the boy to Eli. She said, "Oh, my lord! As your soul lives, my lord, I am the woman who stood here beside you, praying to the Lord. For this boy I prayed, and the Lord has given me my petition which I asked of Him. So I have also dedicated him to the Lord; as long as he lives he is dedicated to the Lord." And he worshiped the Lord there. (vv. 23–28)

And that's the second lesson we learn from Hannah: She kept in mind her promise and gave up her own plans for God's. There are times and occasions in life when God has a unique purpose to fulfill. Along the way He may allow a rare delay or setback—even an obstacle to appear in the path. God didn't respond to Hannah until she made her vow to give back the very thing she wanted most—her son. But she wasn't willing to give up until she reached her desperate situation.

If the Lord has pushed the pause button on your prayers, don't give up. If He has delayed His answer, don't stop trusting. All that means is He is driving you to a point of spiritual depth and experience with Him that goes beyond the norm. He wants to blow your mind with something—to have you see Him reveal something that is beyond the natural in order to accomplish a greater kingdom purpose. Far too often you and I will not open our eyes or our hearts to the depths of the spiritual until things get desperate.

God had a special plan for Hannah's firstborn child, Samuel. Samuel would go on to be an instrumental prophet in the land of the Israelites, affecting both the present and future generations to come. Yet had Hannah not reached a period of utter despair, she may have held on to Samuel for her own gain. Once she did, she surrendered her plans and honored her promise to give.

Sometimes God wants to ask us to let go of something for His sake that we would never let go of except at a point of crisis. Isn't that what He made Abraham do? He asked Abraham to sacrifice his son—his only son through Sarah, the son whom he loved. When Abraham, in faith, gave his son to the Lord, God gave Abraham back his son.

Powerful Prayers Are Giving Prayers

Luke 6:38 is a powerful verse that we often neglect to understand completely, but it directly applies to the fruitfulness and power of our prayers:

KINGDOM PRAYER

Give, and *it* will be given to you. They will pour into your lap a good measure—pressed down, shaken together, and running over. For by your standard of measure *it* will be measured to you in return. (emphasis added)

Notice the word "it" in that verse. That's a very powerful small word. Whatever you are asking God to give to you, give *it* to Him. Whatever the substance of your prayers contains that you want God to do for you, change for you, fix for you—or whatever—see how and where you can do something similar for someone else. Hannah wanted a child so she gave God a child. Abraham wanted his promise of legacy, so he gave God the son through whom that legacy would occur. Give the very *it* that you are seeking and *it* will be given to you. It's a verse in the Scriptures—it's truth. Test it. God is good on His Word.

Are you relationally barren? Then give of yourself relationally to someone else in need, perhaps a shut-in or an elderly person at a group home. Are you financially struggling? Then by all means be generous to someone else in need, as generous as you can. Hand over to God the *it* that you are praying about, and *it* will be given to you.

When you step out in faith and give out of your lack to someone else, you are demonstrating that you believe God when, based on your circumstances, believing God is the last thing you want to do. You are operating on faith even though you can't figure out how your solution will ever come.

Do you need answered prayer? Then seek to be the answer to someone else's prayer. The standard of measure that you give will be the standard of measure you will receive in return, and then some. Bear in mind, God usually outgives us. Hannah didn't just give birth to Samuel. She got more than she asked

86

for. In the next chapter of 1 Samuel—one of two books named after her son—we read that Hannah "conceived and gave birth to three sons and two daughters" (1 Samuel 2:21). Hannah got a houseful after all.

WHEN YOU CAN NO
LONGER ENDURE, SURRENDER

If you are struggling right now in a situation you feel you cannot endure much longer, take heart. Allow yourself to go low, even to the point of weeping bitterly like Hannah, because it is at that point that you will find the freedom to trust God fully. It is at that point you will find the powerful tool called *surrender*. Surrender what you think you desperately need into His hands and providence. When you do, God will give you the strength to keep going in order to reach His perfect plan for your life.

Surrender is a secret to answered prayer. It has opened more doors, and even wombs, than we may even realize. Surrender is letting go of your timing, your will and even your intended purpose and trusting God in His. That is the essence of alignment. That is the DNA of faith. It is also the power found in kingdom prayer.

CHAPTER 7

Two or Three Together

Here are two more racing stories, one noncompetitive, the other a state championship race. In the first, Lance Corporal Myles Kerr held the lead in the annual 5K fun run through the streets of Charlevoix, Michigan, as he and some of his marine friends had pulled out in front of the pack.

Rounding a corner, Myles spotted a nine-year-old boy on a nearby street, yet far back on the winding course. Young Brandon had apparently been separated from the friends he had been running with. Now struggling at the back of the runners, Brandon looked scared and alone.

That's when Myles decided to do what he knew was the right thing to do. He slowed down, then retreated to where Brandon was.

"How you doing, little guy?" the big, strong marine wearing fatigues asked.

Brandon didn't say much at first. And then he turned his head and asked, "Sir, will you please run with me?"

Of course Myles would. After all, as a marine he was trained to leave no (young) man behind. Myles and Brandon ran slowly together throughout the rest of the race, and eventually crossed the finish line together.[1]

Then there was Melanie Bailey, a North Dakota high school senior competing in the 2014 Eastern Dakota Conference Cross Country Championship.

With only a fraction of a mile remaining on this sunny afternoon, one runner went down with a devastating injury to her patella tendon. Danielle LaNoue grabbed her left knee in pain as other runners passed her by. But then knowing this was the end of her high school racing career, she struggled back up to try and finish. Yet her injury proved to be too much. Weeping in pain, she limped as far as she could and then crumpled to the ground, unable to finish on her own.

That's when Melanie caught up with Danielle. "Hop on my back," Melanie urged the crying stranger. This was Melanie's last race too, but she wasn't about to finish it while leaving someone else helpless behind.

Danielle climbed onto the back of Melanie, a girl much smaller than she was. Melanie then slowly carried not only her own weight but the other runner's as well across the finish line. It took eight minutes and thirty seconds longer to cross that line than the winner of the race. But while both girls lost, tied for dead last, both also gained something even greater. They gained grace, a friendship, and hope.[2]

You may be like Heather or Hannah who we looked at in our last chapter, crumpled in your own pain but still able to have the faith you need to get up on your own and carry you through as you continue on your prayer path. If that is you, then I want to encourage you to never give up. Despite the tears, scars, and what other people may say, listen to the announcer calling from heaven, "Watch out for _____" and fill in your name. You're going to make it.

But if your struggles have become too much and if in your tears, you just can't find the way to keep hanging in there and continue praying for something that has gone on for so long, then ask God to send you a Myles or a Melanie today. Someone who will run (pray) with you if you just need the extra company to stay in stride. Or someone who will lift you up and upon whose faith you can hop a ride. I always tell people when their faith is running low to piggyback on someone else's faith who has been through what they have already and gotten to the other side.

> *We were created to live together and even to pray together. God hears our collective prayers.*

There's no shame in needing help in your spiritual journey. Like little Brandon, don't be afraid to ask. We were created to work together, live together, create together, and even to pray together. God hears our collective prayers.

THE POWER OF COLLECTIVE PRAYER

Examples in the Scriptures

Collective kingdom prayer is a power unto its own. Many times throughout Scripture, we witness God responding to the collective cries, groans, praises, and prayers of His people. A cursory glance through the Bible turns up multiple scenarios of people or even an entire nation crying out to God and God hearing their collective prayer. The following are just a few found in the Old Testament:

> Now it came about in *the course of* those many days that the king of Egypt died. And the sons of Israel sighed because of the bondage, and they cried out; and for help because of *their* bondage rose up to God. (Ex. 2:23)

> As Pharaoh drew near, the sons of Israel looked, and behold, the Egyptians were marching after them, and they became very frightened; so the sons of Israel cried out to the Lord. (Ex. 14:10)

> When the sons of Israel cried to the Lord, the Lord raised up a deliverer for the sons of Israel to deliver them. (Judg. 3:9)

> The sons of Israel cried to the Lord. (Judg. 4:3)

> They were helped against them, and the Hagrites and all who were with them were given into their hand; for they cried out to God in the battle, and He answered their prayers because they trusted in Him. (1 Chron. 5:20)

> When Judah turned around, behold, they were attacked both front and rear; so they cried to the Lord, and the priests blew the trumpets. (2 Chron. 13:14)

The New Testament also records times when groups of people gathered together in prayer, especially in Acts:

> They were continually devoting themselves to the apostles' teaching and to fellowship, to the breaking of bread and to prayer. (2:42) And when they heard *this*, they lifted their voices to God with one

accord and said, "O Lord, it is You who made the heaven and the earth and the sea, and all that is in them." (4:24)

And when they had prayed, the place where they had gathered together was shaken, and they were all filled with the Holy Spirit and began to speak the word of God with boldness. (4:31)

When our days there were ended, we left and started on our journey, while they all, with wives and children, escorted us until *we were* out of the city. After kneeling down on the beach and praying, we said farewell to one another. (21:5)

Group and corporate prayer is a frequent occurrence in Scripture. Especially if we were to look at group praise, the examples would be too numerous to mention. Frequently throughout the Bible, groups gathered together to praise God for what He had done, for who He is (His attributes), or for any number of things.

Examples in Our Church

A couple of year ago at the close of one of our Sunday morning services a very powerful event occurred involving corporate prayer and praise. I had preached a message on Jehosophat and his approach to the national battle they were facing. (See 2 Chron. 20:1–25. I'll go into greater detail on this biblical example of group prayer and praise in chapter 15.) As the service ended, I invited the congregation to pray and praise collectively or privately in their seats or at front of the church with the approach we had just looked at in the message.

People came forward by the thousands. Before I knew it the entire front half of the sanctuary was filled with individuals and groups on their knees, prostrate, standing—praying and praising God. It was an awesome moment before the Lord. And like awesome moments before the Lord on Sunday mornings where it is closing in on 1:30 p.m. and lunch schedules are calling, I assumed this one would soon pass. But I couldn't have been more wrong.

Thirty minutes passed. Then an hour. Then nearly two. But the people remained. A few singers had chosen to stay behind as well, having felt led by the Spirit to do so. Long after the service was over and we had officially closed, the power in that room felt just as strong. In fact, it felt stronger. I saw women with women, some with tears running down their faces. Men holding up men's arms and hands, pleading to the Lord on behalf of each other.

It was a unique moment of witnessing the power of corporate prayer and praise. Since that time, I have heard stories from congregation members who were present about how God used that time to bring about a remarkable breakthrough, opened doors, or answered prayers in their lives.

It is good to pray with or near one another. In many ways it encourages each other, and we have been told to encourage each other (e.g., 1 Thess. 5:11, Heb. 3:13). One of the greatest ways to do this is through prayer.

Here's another example. Each year at the beginning of a new year our church holds a weeklong Solemn Assembly. This is a time set aside where every person is challenged to fast (at whatever level he or she feels comfortable) and commit the week to the Lord in prayer for guidance, breakthroughs, clarity, and praise. During the Wednesday night service of that Solemn Assembly week, we gather as a congregation for a time of praying *with* one another and *for* one another. The service is scheduled to last an hour and a half but rarely have we ended on time. It is an electric yet also somber evening where you can sense the fullness of God's presence among us as we devote our words and our hearts to God through group prayer.

THE NEED FOR COMMUNITY PRAYER—AND ACTION

Our Need for a Joshua and a Hur

We need each other. One of the greatest ways we can be there for each other is through prayer. It's not always easy to keep the faith in the face of repeated disappointment. Those are the times when we need someone to come alongside us and hold up our arms, similar to how Aaron and Hur did for Moses when Moses waged a spiritual war in the heavenlies (a method of prayer) as Joshua and the army battled in the valley below. Moses explained the strategy for this battle in Exodus where we read that he said to Joshua,

> "Choose men for us and go out, fight against Amalek. Tomorrow I will station myself on the top of the hill with the staff of God in my hand." Joshua did as Moses told him, and fought against Amalek; and Moses, Aaron, and Hur went up to the top of the hill. So it came about when Moses held his hand up, that Israel prevailed, and when he let his hand down, Amalek prevailed. (Ex. 17:8–11)

The winning or losing of this battle would not be determined by those fighting in the physical realm. Who would win and who would lose would not rest on what Joshua and his men would do. Rather, it was on what Moses would do with God in the spiritual realm—whether he could keep his staff raised, or whether it got lowered. How they fared in the valley was not tied to their physical strength; instead it was inextricably tied to Moses' intercession on the mountain. The battle would be fought, and won, spiritually.

Our Need for Action

But that didn't mean Joshua and his men were to sit down and drink tea. They still had to do their part. Kingdom prayer must be coupled with kingdom action.

It is only in understanding that you must bring both the valley and the mountain together that victory in prayer will be experienced. As a believer in Christ and a follower of God, you have a responsibility to do all that you can do in challenges and trials that you face. Yet unless God also supports and engages in the victory, it will not be enough. As you pray, ask the Lord what action steps He also wants you to take.

On one hand, God is going to fix it. Yet on the other hand, you must do all God commands of you to fix it, too, often with the help of fellow believers through prayer.

As Paul writes, "We then, as workers together *with* him" (2 Cor. 6:1a, emphasis added).

There must always be a balance between what God does on the mountain and what you or I are responsible for in the valley. We are to never excuse irresponsibility in the name of God. Yet we are also to look to personal responsibility as sufficient to achieve all that God wants to do in the midst of our conflicts, battles, and wars.

When We Sigh and Become Weary

Give Emotional Support

Spiritual battles can be tiresome. Trust me; I know that as well as you. As Moses held the rod high on the hill, his "hands were heavy" (Ex. 17:12). He grew weary and the weight began to accumulate. It's not that the staff weighed any more than it did at the start, it's just that he had held it up for so long that it felt heavier than before. It's like those times when your prayer journal or prayer closet records the same need for so long that when you start to pray for it, you sigh. You feel burdened and you need encouragement and strength.

This is what happened to Moses, and as he lost strength his arms began to fall. Yet as his arms fell, the battle down below fell to pieces. So Aaron and Hur came up with a plan:

> Then they took a stone and put it under him, and he sat on it; and Aaron and Hur supported his hands, one on one side and one on the other. Thus his hands were steady until the sun set. So Joshua overwhelmed Amalek and his people with the edge of the sword. (Ex. 17:12–13)

Aaron and Hur's job became that of supporting Moses's hands. It was their job to join the spiritual battle with him. They entered into the realm of the invisible by giving their friend and leader strength. We do the same when we gather together with others to pray or even when we pray for one another in what is called intercessory prayer.

Listen and Remind of God's Victory

A man in our church came to my house one afternoon. His

head was down and hands were limp at his side. He was tired and looked distraught.

We sat together for about an hour as he shared the different challenges life kept throwing his way. I didn't solve them for him. I didn't bail him out of any situation. But what I did do was remind him of the spiritual nature of the battle. I reminded him of God's victory, power, and His presence. I prayed with him and for him, entering into the spiritual battle because his strength was gone.

Sometimes we just need an Aaron or a Hur to help us connect again with heaven. Because when you lose contact with the spiritual, you easily become defeated in the physical. Yet when you maintain contact with the spiritual, you prevail in the valleys of life.

Some of us are throwing in the towel when we have never raised the rod. Joshua fought in the valley; Moses on the hill, and because of it, "Joshua overwhelmed Amalek and his people with the edge of the sword" (v. 13). They won. Life's battles and challenges aren't meant to be faced alone. Yes, there are times of quiet and solitude—there are those times like Elijah had that God calls you by yourself to the brook or you face Baal and his followers alone. But there are also those times God brings us together to support each other, and one of the primary ways we do this is through collective kingdom prayer.

THE POWER OF TWO OR THREE

Group prayer carries with it great kingdom authority. As Jesus said, "Again I say to you, that if two of you agree on earth about anything that they may ask, it shall be done for them by My Father who is in heaven. For where two or three have gathered together in My name, I am there in their midst" (Matt. 18:19–20).

The context of this powerful passage is Jesus talking about accountability within the body of Christ. In the earlier verses, He speaks on how we are to approach each other when a brother or sister is living in open sin. He also mentions that whatever we bind on earth is bound in heaven, and whatever is loosed on earth is loosed in heaven (v.18), which means to access and exercise kingdom authority. Mixed within mutual accountability and heavenly accessibility with regard to authority comes these words on group prayer.

The context is critical in understanding these verses fully because when Christ spoke about accountability for a believer, He said if the believer does not turn from the sin, then bring along someone else, or multiple people, to address it, "so that by the mouth of two or three witnesses every fact may be confirmed" (v. 16b). The phrase "two or three witnesses" is an Old Testament phrase. In Deuteronomy 19:15 we read, "A single witness shall not rise up against a man on account of any iniquity or any sin which he has committed; on the evidence of two or three witnesses a matter shall be confirmed."

Later Moses called on both heaven and earth as two witnesses to his statement to the children of Israel, declaring, "I call heaven and earth to witness against you today, that I have set before you life and death, the blessing and the curse. So choose life in order that you may live, you and your descendants" (Deut. 30:19).

Likewise in Deuteronomy 17:6, Moses declared, "On the evidence of two witnesses or three witnesses, he who is to die shall be put to death; he shall not be put to death on the evidence of one witness." When Jesus mentions that "if two of you agree on earth about anything," He is reaching back to the Old Testament to tell the church something about the New Testament days. Two or three witnesses were used in legal courts. They were used as a legislative authority to make decisions and to declare what would be. When two or three gathered in the Old Testament times with regard to a matter, it wasn't just to shake hands, sing songs, and fellowship. No, this structure was designed to make something official. That's important to note—the backdrop of Jesus using this term within the context of the passage is the backdrop of legal witnesses deciding together what would be.

Looking more deeply at the passage, we also see that the Greek word used for "agree" is the word from which we get our English term "symphony." It means to "sound together." Another way of describing it is to "say the same thing." Have you ever heard the phrase "we are on the same page"? It's said often in conversations, meetings or emails to denote when two or more people get to the place where they see things the same way and agree upon the desired outcome.

Thus the key to answered prayer when it comes to group prayer is this symphonic orchestration of being on the same page, of one accord. It is not only praying with one another but also believing, thinking, and desiring in cadence. Not just cognitively but at the heart and faith level. When two or more people agree on anything which God has authorized to be bound or loosed (in alignment under God), and they ask for it—it will be done. It will come about. I've seen it in my own life on numbers of occasions, but it is not as simple as it sounds. This is because the key is being on one accord. Being in agreement—sharing a like-mindedness and level of faith on the matter. The key is spiritual unity under the Lordship of Jesus Christ since He is in the midst.

That is why one of Satan's primary weapons in spiritual warfare is to create disunity. Whether that happens through relational spats, disagreements, increasing selfish desires, or any number of ways, Satan desires to keep us disunified and separated from the authority of Jesus Christ. If successful, he can keep us disengaged on any real level in the spiritual realm. He can keep our prayers powerless.

> *When two or more people agree on anything which God has authorized— and they ask for it —it will be done.*

Being spiritually in sync with each other is a key to accessing heavenly authority. Yet becoming spiritually in sync requires a level of mutual humility, submission, selflessness, love, and deference that is rare. That is why we do not see the results of group prayers at the level in which we should see them. Even, sadly enough, in our marriages and in our homes.

God even tells husbands in 1 Peter 3:7 that if they are not in alignment with their wife on all levels, they might as well not pray. We read, "You husbands in the same way, live with *your wives* in an understanding way . . . and show her honor as a fellow heir of the grace of life, so that your prayers will not be hindered." Men, if you are not showing your wife honor, your prayers will be hindered. If you are dismissive to her needs, your prayers will be hindered. Effective prayer hinges far greater on our relationships with others and our relationship with God than on how much time we spend in our prayer closets or on our knees.

To be in "symphony" with one another is required for our group prayers to reach heaven's ears with one sound. Until we are in alignment under God's principles of loving Him and loving others and submitting to His authority, our prayers will make as much sense to the Lord as an orchestra does to us when it is warming up and not operating under the authority of the conductor. Only when we pray in one accord will we experience the power kingdom prayer was designed to provide.

CHAPTER 8

Commitment and Calm

Spiderman, Batman, Superman, and Iron Man. America is obsessed with superheroes. No matter how many sequels come out, theaters overflow with fans waiting to see how their superhero will save the day. What is it about these "heroes" that so captivates our attention?

In a world so wrought with problems—injustice, oppression, too much power in the hands of evil men—it is nice to escape to a place where power lies in the hands of selfless men and women who can make a difference.

But while this makes for an interesting plot in comic books, movies, and TV shows, it is not reality. All of those powers are make-believe, total fiction. And we, the ordinary people, are left holding the bag while the world is seemingly overrun by evil. What we need are real-life heroes, real people who have made a real difference. These are people who understand the power of prayer—and use it.

The Bible tells the stories of countless men and women who were not extraordinary because of special powers or abilities, but simply because God gave them His Spirit to carry out His plan to overcome the evil around them. God gave them insight into communicating with Him and because of that, they were able to do more than most.

THE LIFE AND TIMES OF ELIJAH

The prophet Elijah was such a man. Elijah has multiple stories recorded about him (and we'll look at other situations of his in later chapters). Like a trilogy of a popular movie plot—Elijah shows up again and again.

Elijah wasn't "destined for greatness" like Clark Kent or Peter Parker, but he was called out and designed to accomplish God's purposes in his generation. Elijah was from the hick town of Tishbe, a no-nothing place. His family wasn't famous, and he didn't possess extraordinary strength or knowledge. All he had was his name.

In the Old Testament, names meant more than they do today. A person's name told the world who he was and what he believed. Elijah's name means: "Yahweh is my God." When Elijah's parents named him, they instilled faith in him—faith in the only living, powerful God.

Living under an Evil Leader

But Elijah grew up in a world overrun by evil, much like ours today. From the time of his childhood, he watched king after king do evil in the sight of the Lord (1 Kings 16:25, 30). None of them kept God's law but instead led God's people further and further away from Him.

When Elijah first appears in Scripture (17:1), Ahab is king and Jezebel is his wife. This is what the Bible has to say about these two leaders of Israel: "Ahab did more to provoke the Lord

God of Israel than all the kings of Israel who were before him
. . . there was no one like Ahab who sold himself to do evil in
the sight of the Lord, because Jezebel his wife incited him"
(1 Kings 16:33; 21:25). Superman's enemy Lex Luther has nothing on Ahab!

Idolatry, indulgence, and moral depravity had become law in
Israel during Elijah's days. Ahab allowed his foreign wife, Jezebel,
to institute Baal worship, turning people away from Yahweh.

Today, American culture does not physically bend its knee
to foreign gods, but we are still a nation of great idolatry. It seems
we worship everything but God: money, sex, power, image . . .
and as far as indulgence and moral depravity go, well, they too
have become our idols. God chose Elijah to be His messenger
of judgment and call His people back to Himself. Empowering
Elijah to perform miracles, speak without fear in the face of evil
and declare boldly the word of the Lord, God made Elijah a true
hero, a man we can look up to and learn from.

Elijah's life was not a leisurely walk in the park. He was not
spared suffering just because he was God's man. Quite the con-
trary, God put Elijah through years of trials to strengthen his
faith. But it was these hardships that prepared him for the more
difficult days of faith that would redefine him as a true hero of
the faith.

Preparing for a Great Challenge: Alone with God

When God brought Elijah to the pinnacle of his ministry,
literally on the top of a mountain, God had increased his faith
and filled him with His Spirit so that he was ready to stand up
for truth, no matter the cost. One of the ways God prepared
Elijah was through a time of solitude. Far too many of us today

have neglected the virtue and discipline of spending time with God. Our lives are busy, distracting, and noisy. But often God speaks to us in the quiet and stillness of life, and that requires times of solitude, reflection, meditation, and learning.

Before Elijah performed one of his greatest feats—confronting and humbling hundreds of false prophets—God would lead the prophet into a time alone with Him. Elijah had just given an extraordinary warning to King Ahab: neither rain nor dew would grace the land (1 Kings 17:1). Soon after that the Lord told the prophet to leave the land: "Turn eastward, and hide yourself by the brook Cherith, which is east of the Jordan" (v. 2).

In other words, God was telling Elijah to leave the bright lights of the castle, the busy activity in Israel, and go to the brook of Cherith to hide for a little while. The meaning of solitude is simply to enter into God's rest. It's setting aside time with God so that you clearly understand what He is saying as well as what you are thinking and believing. That's what Elijah did.

Solitude can bring clarity to your own thoughts when you remove yourself from the distractions of living in a world that is constantly inundated. Television, mobile phones bringing calls on the go and text messages, doctor appointments and daily duties, and much more can consume and distract us.

Getting alone with God is essential to hear His voice. Many of us don't know what we're doing or why we're doing it because we haven't stopped long enough to hear from God or to even consider our motivations. One of the repeated themes in the book of Hebrews is finding (or entering) the rest of God, and it can give us insight into why Elijah was sent away to the brook. The writer of Hebrews says,

Therefore, let us fear if, while a promise remains of entering His rest, any one of you may seem to have come short of it. . . . For if Joshua had given them rest, He would not have spoken of another day after that. So there remains a Sabbath rest for the people of God. (Heb. 4:1, 8–9)

A Time of Rest and Worship

Perhaps a review of the meaning of the Sabbath will also clarify this concept of rest. Genesis tells us that God created everything in six days. When He finished with everything, He called it very good. But on the seventh day, He rested (Gen. 2:2).

Now, God didn't rest because He was tired. After all, how hard have you worked if you've only spoken things into existence? God rested because He had finished His work in the time frame He had allotted Himself to do it. The purpose of God's rest was to enjoy His creation—to sit back, look at what He had made, and relish His handiwork.

The concept of rest was no small issue in the Old Testament. Keeping the Sabbath was one of the Ten Commandments (Ex. 20:9–11), "a time when you shall not do any work, you or your son or your daughter" (v. 10).

In Old Testament times the Sabbath was a day when you wouldn't try to create anything. To rest was to reflect on your achievements for the past six days. It was also a time of enjoying God and devoting yourself to worship of your creator. God never wanted Israel to lose sight of the concept of rest.

Friend, you can't find out what God's plan is until you have spent time in His presence, enjoying and worshiping Him. And you can't spend time in His presence if you are always so busy doing other things. You have to pull aside in solitude and listen to His voice.

When I think about the importance of solitude, I think about Jesus. He led a very busy life. He always had someone to heal, someone to save, some problem to fix, some disciple to correct. It was a busy life, and Jesus worked hard. Yet even Jesus took time to be alone with God (Matt. 14:23, Luke 6:12, Mark 6:31). Jesus wants us to spend time in solitude because that's where rejuvenation takes place for what God has in store for us. Satan's best weapon against the church is distractions—things that keep us from the rest God intends for us to experience. Things that keep us from communicating with God. That's why Satan tries his best to keep us from the quietness of God's presence, so that we're unable to hear God's voice and we lose our own desire to talk to Him as well.

Preparing in a Quiet Place

God's word to Elijah was to go to the brook of Cherith. A brook is not a spectacular place to go, but God doesn't require us to meet Him in some fancy place. He just wants us to meet with Him. It needs to be a place of quiet, a place where we can focus. When you want to be alone with God, you need a place that's isolated, a place that can be quiet. You want a place where there is enough stillness that if the Holy Spirit has something unique to say to you about a decision, a direction, or a relationship, you will be able to hear it in your spirit. The writer of Hebrews puts it this way, "For the word of God is living and active and sharper than any two-edged sword, and piercing as far as the division of soul and spirit, of both joints and marrow" (Heb. 4:12).

When the writer says "the word of God," he's using the

Greek word *rhema*, which refers to the spoken word of God as opposed to just the written Word of God. He's saying that when you enter God's rest with an open Bible, with the purpose of hearing God's voice in prayer, God will make a distinction between your soul and your spirit.

This is important because your soul is your personality. It's who you are as a distinct individual. Our bodies reflect the differences of the soul, and the spirit—which is even deeper—is how we communicate with God.

Now, many people have asked, "How do I know if what I'm hearing is from me or from God?" Hebrews 4:12 answers this question. When God speaks, He will divide your soul and your spirit. He will let you know if He's the one doing the talking. If you'll just enter God's rest, He'll speak into your spirit so that you'll know you weren't just hearing from yourself.

God does speak today, and He confirms His voice with two or three witnesses. I'm not saying necessarily that God speaks in an audible voice, but He speaks to our spirits.

THE PURPOSE OF SOLITUDE

We've seen that God can speak to us today, and we've seen that He wants us to find solitude. But why is solitude important? Why does God want us to "go to the brook" and find solitude? The answer is to get a fresh word from Him, that He might develop our Christian character for the new challenges ahead.

Before you face the new challenges ahead or face that big decision in your life, you'd better stay by the

> *Solitude allows you to hear God's supernatural voice.*

brook. Before you face the enemies of God who want to do you in, you'd better stay by the brook. My friend, don't forget that God has a fresh word for you today, and you receive that word in prayer.

Solitude allows you to hear God's supernatural voice. When Elijah took the initiative to stand for God in front of King Ahab, God took the initiative to tell Elijah to go to the brook; Elijah's work had just begun. Whenever God puts you in a situation where you need to find a place of solitude, you can know that He has something planned for you just beyond the horizon. That's why He needs you to go away with Him and refresh, recharge, and reconnect with Him. God will never send you to the brook to a time of solitude to waste your time. God's request for your special presence with Him is always strategically planned in order to accomplish a kingdom purpose.

After Elijah's time at the brook, he had an important assignment. He was now ready for this powerful moment in his life and the life of the nation in which he lived because he had spent time alone with God. We read as the passage continues that Elijah then went to the top of Mount Carmel for a face-off between Elijah's God and the god of the king.

FROM SOLITUDE TO THE MOUNTAINTOP

The Battle on Mount Carmel

On the top of Mount Carmel, all by himself, Elijah represented God before King Ahab, Jezebel, 450 prophets of Baal, and the whole nation of Israel. It was a showdown, a once-and-for-all face-off between the two warring gods of Israel, Yahweh and Baal.

The test was simple: after the prophets prepared a calf

for sacrifice upon an altar, whichever god could send fire from heaven to light the sacrifice would be the real God. If you don't know the rest of this story, here's how the two-round battle went. First the prophets of Baal entered the ring:

> They . . . called on the name of Baal from morning until noon, saying, "O Baal, answer us." But there was no voice and no one answered. And they leaped about the altar which they had made. . . . They cried with a loud voice and cut themselves . . . with swords and lances until the blood gushed out on them. When midday was past, they raved until the time of the offering of the evening sacrifice; but there was no voice, no one answered, and no one paid attention. (1 Kings 18:26–29)

Round 1: Baal—0.

Then Elijah repaired the altar of the Lord that was in disrepair and dug a trench around it, added wood, and placed the sacrifice on the altar. Next he had the people pour four pitchers of water onto the burnt offering and the wood. They poured the four pitchers two more times until the water flowed around the altar. Then "he also filled the trench with water" (v. 35). Finally he prayed, "O Lord, the God of Abraham, Isaac and Israel, today let it be known that You are God in Israel and that I am Your servant and I have done all these things at Your word. Answer me, O Lord, answer me, that this people may know that You, O Lord, are God" (vv. 36–37). And God answered that prayer:

> Then the fire of the Lord fell and consumed the burnt offering, and the wood and the stones and the dust, and licked up the water that was in the trench. When all the people saw it, they fell on their faces; and they said, "The Lord, He is God; the Lord, He is God!" (vv. 38–39)

Round 2: Yahweh—1. God wins!

Talk about a heroic event. There stood Ahab, along with hundreds of false prophets who had been leading the people astray for years. And then there was Elijah—one man, unafraid, with enough faith to rebuke his whole nation for idolatry and call down the very fire of God. Elijah, a man of no reputation, a man tried in the fires of life, an ordinary man, not special in any way except that God decided to use him during one of the darkest seasons of history for His people. He is not unlike you or me . . . yet he became a real hero, designed and used by God.

Elijah's Commitment to God

This is what it means to be a man or woman of God. This is what it means to understand the power of prayer. A lot of us feel that the power of prayer is in what we say, where we pray, or how long we pray. We fail to realize that a lot of the power comes in who we are and what we do. Elijah demonstrated commitment before the Lord in actions that showed he believed God was telling the truth and would be faithful. Elijah wasn't praying as he built the altar. He wasn't praying when he had the water poured over it. He was working. Yet the DNA within his work and his actions reflected a heart of faith. Thus, when he did eventually pray, God responded immediately and heroically.

Notice that Elijah never claimed the glory for himself. In his heroism, he pointed us to the source of his strength, power, and ability—Yahweh. He pointed us to the true Hero in our midst— God Himself.

When you or I tap into God's power, we access the authority that spoke the world into existence, parted the sea from the land, created life itself, and raised the dead. That's true power.

And that is what is available to you and me through the understanding and application of this method of communicating called prayer.

In prayer, we have access not only to God the Father, but intercession through God the Son and access to the power of the Holy Spirit within us. Through prayer, we can defeat the enemy, release the captives, and bring peace to chaos in our own lives, families, churches, and communities.

Prayer opens up the floodgates for His kingdom power to flow in and through us.

CHAPTER 9

Stop Blocking Your Miracle

A few months ago eleven people stood trapped in an office elevator in Bermuda. I was one of them. If you have ever been stuck in an elevator, you know it is not a comfortable situation to be in.

Particularly if the elevator does not have a phone, which this one did not.

It happened to be a Saturday night as well, so the chance of finding available help walking by in the building was slim. Soon the air began to thin, as the eleven of us remained as still as we could—breathing as lightly as we could. Unable to communicate with anyone outside the elevator, we waited, feeling all the more desperate as time dragged on. Tick-tock. Tick-tock. The minutes felt like months.

Everyone was doing all they could to try and remain calm, but it was clear that the longer it was taking to become free, the more uncomfortable everyone was getting, including myself. We were in a situation we could not escape, encased in a scenario we could not remedy.

We tried to pull the elevator doors apart. But they were too thick, too heavy. The steel was too strong and the closing was too tight.

We could not release ourselves from the predicament no matter how hard we tried. What we needed was someone on the outside who had the knowledge and power to open up something we were unable to do. To put it another way, our natural capacity was limited; we needed someone who had a greater capacity do for us what we could not do for ourselves.

Eventually, after nearly an hour, we got free when one of the individual's cellphones somehow managed to get a signal for a brief moment and he called the fire department. But the uncomfortable incident revealed to me a spiritual lesson that would stay with me for days, even weeks after.

What happened to us that night reminded me of what has happened to so many people—that feeling of being trapped. Maybe not literally in an elevator on a Saturday night, but they are trapped by their circumstances, or an addiction; it could even be by an unhealthy relationship. They don't want to be there, but the doors to freedom simply won't open on their own. Nor can they pry them open.

They need help from outside themselves, but due to static on their lines or the lack of a clear signal they are not getting through to that help. What they need requires an intimate, abiding, and obedient relationship with God. A lot of us have not seen God come through simply because we are holding God up ourselves. We are either delaying or denying His supernatural presence in our situation by failing to make contact through prayers prayed in faith, fervency, and trust from a kingdom perspective.

PRAYER AND OBEDIENCE

Often we narrow the efficacy of our prayers down to one thing: faith. Instead, we neglect to realize that multiple elements go into making prayers effective. Two elements we have just explored in Elijah's prayer on Mount Carmel (and echoed in James 5:16 [NKJV]) are fervency and righteousness. Now, captured in a dramatic story in John 11, we find a third element for authoritative prayers that advance God's kingdom on earth: obedience.

Most who have been believers for any length of time can recite the story of Jesus raising Lazarus from the dead. What is often emphasized in the retelling of this story is the power of Christ to raise the dead coupled with the compassion of Christ in that He wept at the sight of His distressed friends. In addition, the delay of our Savior in coming to the tomb (John 11:17–21) reveals a glimpse into God's somewhat unconventional timing.

But one aspect of this story is often overlooked, yet it is one of the fundamental components to effective kingdom prayer. It is this aspect of obedience.

When we do not act on what God has said, we limit ourselves, and God. We block Him from doing miracles in our lives and the lives of others. But obedience birthed in faith unleashes God's power. So let's journey to Lazarus's tomb.

OBEDIENCE AT LAZARUS'S TOMB

Let's start our look at this story shortly after the shortest verse in the Bible, "Jesus wept" (v. 35). We come on the scene to find Jesus crying; he shares in the pain of His friends Martha and Mary. But let me point out something about Jesus' emotions. While Jesus sympathizes with our infirmities, He never lets His emotions govern His theology. He can feel our pain and even feel pain for us but how He feels about a situation won't determine what He does, because His commitment to God's truth and will override any emotions at the moment. So while Jesus is moved by the scenario and anguished by the situation, He doesn't look for a quick fix. Instead He seeks to address the problem within the predicament.

> God will often seek to involve us in His answers to prayer as a way of testing our trust.

Rather than raise Lazarus immediately on His own, Jesus engages Martha in the miracle He is about to perform. In verses 38 and 39 we read, "Jesus, again being deeply moved within, came to the tomb. Now it was a cave, and a stone was lying against it. Jesus said, 'Remove the stone.'"

Jesus—through whom the world was created—did not need help moving the stone. In fact, a stone could not keep Him in the grave, even upon His own death. So Jesus didn't need the stone removed to raise His friend from the dead.

But that's exactly why He asked. God will often seek to involve us in His answers to prayer as a way of revealing our faith, testing our trust, and giving us experience in exercising our role in accessing kingdom authority. Which is precisely what He did with Martha. And Martha did what most of us do—she didn't respond well.

She argued.

She hesitated.

She reasoned.

She rationalized.

Essentially, she refused.

Verse 39 says, "Martha, the sister of the deceased, said to Him, 'Lord, by this time there will be a stench, for he has been dead four days.'"

Replacing Logic with Faith

Jesus had said, "Remove the stone." Martha had replied, in a summary of words, "Just a minute, Jesus. What You have asked is impractical and illogical." After which Martha went on to insult Jesus' intelligence by implying that He—who made life—evidently didn't know how death worked. Her reply came couched with a lesson in mortuary science, an explanation of how decomposition occurred. Martha made sure Jesus realized that rigor mortis had already set in, the cells had been denied their oxygen and gases were released through decomposition. Bottom line: the body stunk.

Please don't skip over this reality of Martha's response. Everything she said was true. She was not delusional. Neither had she been deceived. Martha was absolutely accurate in her analysis. If it had been a biology course, she would have gotten an A. But this wasn't Biology 101—this was a lesson in faith. And faith often requires us to set logic aside in order to experience the supernatural overriding the natural.

Martha simply argued back in a way that, from a physical standpoint, might be absolutely correct but from a spiritual standpoint has no bearing at all.

That's why paying attention to Jesus' response to Martha can help us all experience greater kingdom authority in our own prayer lives. Listen to these words as if Christ is speaking directly to you, "Did I not say to you that if you believe, you will see the glory of God?" (v. 40). His answer was simple yet profound. Jesus never wastes His words. Jesus was exact in His response to Martha, just as He is exact in His response to us. He addressed the root of the problem—her need to believe—not the reality they were facing. The root and the reality are frequently not the same thing.

Maybe you can compare this situation to a time when a child, niece, or nephew of yours questioned a decision you made. As the adult, you were aware of much more than they were, so when they questioned your decision, your response was simple, "Didn't you hear what I just said?" No discussion. No entering into their concerns. You merely emphasized the point that you had already spoken.

Jesus did the exact same thing with Martha at the tomb. Basically, He told her, "What I am talking about and what you are talking about are not the same thing." Thankfully, Martha got the message and moved the stone. But let's not miss the key lesson of Lazarus: Miracles don't depend on facts; they depend on faith. Sometimes you have to set the facts aside in order to demonstrate faith so you can witness the truth. Sometimes, no matter how bad the object smells, you must move the stone.

Moving beyond Discussion to Obedience

Talking about moving the stone will accomplish nothing. Praying about why you don't want to move the stone will avail nothing. Discussing a dead situation will never make it come to life—only God can do that. That's why when you find yourself trapped as I was in an elevator with no room to move, little air to breathe, and no one to call out to, finding a signal on your phone—or a "line to heaven"—is your only option. That line often requires obedience.

When we argue with God as Martha did, Jesus' response to her is the same to us, "What you are saying has nothing to do with what I just said. I didn't invite you to discuss it—I told you to move the stone."

Friend, nothing will block the supernatural movement of God in your life like logic. Some of us have simply educated ourselves out of the supernatural realm—we have become "too smart" for God, too intelligent for heaven, too brilliant for the kingdom. And because of this brilliance we have missed out on experiencing the miraculous.

Too many believers live by the creed of Missouri, known as the Show Me State. They say to God, "Show me and I'll believe." But God says, "Believe and you will see." What will we see? Jesus said clearly that we will see the "glory of God." The glory of God is God revealing Himself as God in human circumstances. It is God on display, placing His attributes on a billboard big enough that you cannot miss. God allows you to witness Him at work above your circumstances, not in them and definitely not under them. You get to see His kingdom in action.

> *Many believers say to God, "Show me and I'll believe." But God says, "Believe and you will see."*

The true measure of your faith is when you do actions of obedience that reveal you believe God to be telling the truth. Another way to say that is: Faith is acting like God is telling the truth. Faith isn't singing praise songs at church. Neither is it being an usher or leading a small group. Those things are good and those things are profitable—but when it comes to demonstrating your faith during big challenges in your life, faith involves feet that do what God says to do.

You measure your faith by your feet, not by your feelings. Faith includes obeying God even, or especially, when what He says goes against your human understanding. Far too many believers are blocking their miracles by allowing human thought to trump God. They are living like the residents of Nazareth did when Jesus visited his hometown. The apostle Matthew wrote that Jesus "did not do many miracles there because of their unbelief" (Matt. 13:58).

Read those words again and let it sink in: *He did not do many miracles there because of their unbelief.*

You and I are limited to the natural when we live in unbelief. That is, when we do not act on what God has said—whether we understand it or not, figure it out or not, like it or not. We limit ourselves, and God, limited belief shown in our unwillingness to obey.

Do His Revealed Will First

Let me tell you something about the will of God. God has a revealed will, declared to us in the Scriptures. He also has a secret will. As we read in Deuteronomy 29:29, "The secret things belong to the Lord our God." There are many things—more than we could even imagine—that God has not revealed to us. He does reveal those "secret things" from time to time at His own discretion. They surely surprise us. Sometimes, they involve supernatural acts on our behalf or on behalf of those we know—we call them miracles. But here is an important point: You cannot get to God's secret will if you first ignore His revealed will. In other words, if He says to move the stone (that is, whatever you are facing in your particular situation), you have to obey that first before you see what He does behind the stone.

In everyday language, if you are experiencing tension at work with another coworker who is treating you unfairly, you will never see God overrule and override the situation until you obey what He has already revealed. God has already revealed a number of things about this situation.

You may wonder what his revealed will includes. Here are just three aspects, all declared in the New Testament:

> "But I say to you who hear, love your enemies, do good to those who hate you." (Luke 6:27)

> But the fruit of the Spirit is love, joy, peace, patience, kindness, goodness, faithfulness, gentleness, self-control; against such things there is no law. (Gal. 5:22–23)

> Be kind to one another, tender-hearted, forgiving each other, just as God in Christ also has forgiven you. (Eph. 4:32)

From those three passages it is clear we are to display love to those who oppose us, display the nine fruit of the Holy Spirit, and show kindness, compassion, and forgiveness. That right there is enough to keep you busy for a while.

Yes, responding to someone in those ways who is intentionally and unfairly seeking to make your life miserable might make as much sense as removing a stone after someone has been dead for four days. But that's the point. God often doesn't make sense; but He does make miracles. Especially when our hearts, spirits, and actions are aligned with His revealed will. Return kindness for insult, love for aloofness, and blessing for betrayal, and you just may see a miracle.

God has given us plenty in His revealed will that we far too often forget in our prayers. We may spend hours wrestling in prayer, begging God and telling Him every reason why He should answer us, yet all the while neglecting to do what He has already told us to do. So while we are waiting on Him to answer us, He is waiting on us to obey Him. And let me tell you something very important with regard to waiting: The One who exists from eternity to eternity has the ability to wait the longest. God will wait while you wrestle with what He has already told you to do.

We may never know how God is going to change it, reverse it, undo it, or even resurrect it. That is unimportant. Just do what He says to do. Then let Him handle the *how*.

BEING THANKFUL BEFORE THE FACT

Jesus knew the power of kingdom prayer and modeled it for us in raising Lazarus from the dead. But He also modeled something else, something I don't want you to miss. It is a key element in answered prayer. We discover it in *how* Jesus modeled kingdom prayer.

He prayed, "Father, I thank You that You have heard Me. I knew that You always hear Me; but because of the people standing around I said it, so that they may believe that You sent Me" (vv. 41–42). Jesus used that opportunity to amplify what He already knew to those around Him. He knew that God heard every prayer He said. He also knew God would give Him whatever He asked since He was directly in alignment with God. Jesus knew that God was about to raise Lazarus from the grave. But in order that those around Him, as well as us so many years later, would benefit from this truth, He made that statement aloud in His prayer, and He used the past tense. This is Jesus' intercessory work in action.

Before the miracle occurred, Jesus thanked God for having heard—He thanked Him as if the future were already past. That's confidence. Christ was thankful before the fact. You and I should apply the same approach to what we pray and how we pray. Remember, God is moved by faith because kingdom prayer is drawing down from heaven what God has already planned for earth.

The supernatural miracle that is in God's will for your life has already been agreed upon in the spiritual realm. That means you do not have to beg God to do something that is in His will to do. All you need to do is move the stone and thank Him in advance for what He has already determined to do. This is kingdom prayer in action in order to touch heaven and change earth.

When you feel trapped like Lazarus, bound in a dark situation with the only hope being that of divine intervention, listen for God's instruction. Then trust and obey. As 2 Corinthians 6:1 says, we are "workers together with Him." God didn't raise Lazarus from the dead until Martha agreed to move the stone, even though she had previously prayed for healing, and Jesus thanked Him publicly for what He had determined to do. That miracle was a group effort, as most miracles are. Keep that in mind the next time you are praying for God to do that which is beyond you. Listen for His voice, and obey.

CHAPTER 10

Pushing Through in Prayer

Prayer is a vital tool in the hand and heart of every believer. Yet it is a tool we frequently fail to use. Maybe because we don't believe how important it is. Or maybe we doubt how God has established His creation to work regarding prayer.

Many of us, because we think praying must be done a certain way, at a certain time, for a certain length of time, and about certain things, barely pray at all. But it's not about how long you pray as much as it is about demonstrating faith as you pray.

Prayer is the mechanism God has decreed for Him to release what He intends. Prayer never makes God do what He hadn't planned to do, but it can open His hand to do what He determined He would do. Consider it like an exchange. When you put your money into a bank account, it is yours. Even though it is not with you, in your pocket or in your purse. The money in the account is yours.

Many of us will carry a bank debit card instead of cash these days. It's convenient. We don't have to count it out. We can use it almost everywhere we go. The bank card is the point of access between you and your funds. In order to buy your cup of coffee, fill up your gas tank, or get those running shoes at the store, you have to give the person doing the transaction your card. Even if you had a million dollars in your bank account and you wanted a bottle of water at the grocery store, you would still have to hand over, or swipe, your card. You would have to access that which is yours.

We don't typically discuss, ponder, or even fuss about paying for our items with our bank card. We understand it is simply how the system works. Yet with prayer, even though God has established a system that He has told us about and demonstrated for us countless times, we still stand confused and marvel at what our part is to play in the whole thing. We ask such questions as:

- If God intended to give me this child, why do I have to pray to get pregnant when I'm having trouble conceiving?

- If God intended to provide this job, why did I have to ask Him for it?

- Do I need to pray about my sick family member? Doesn't God know we want Him to heal him/her?

I could probably create a list as long as this book of questions that run through our minds with regard to prayer. But if our bank intended to release the funds for us to buy that bottle of water at the grocery store all along, then why do we still need to swipe our card? That's a question rarely, if ever, asked. Because that's a truth we have come to accept. Prayer, as a relational and transactional engagement with God, is a truth that we would do well to come to accept. It's just the way He has set things up.

The truth is: *Prayer activates the decree and will of God.*

WHY WAS ELIJAH'S PRAYER EFFECTIVE?

No other story in the Bible demonstrates this as much as the one we are going to look at in this chapter. It's by far one of my favorite passages to preach on, for it is a visual demonstration of one of life's most powerful principles. God, knowing that for centuries we would struggle in this area called prayer, has painted a portrait of the process of prayer through a drought, a man, a cloud, a rainstorm, and some fruit. We have already met the man Elijah in chapter 8. Elijah may have been a prophet, but he was a normal human, with "a nature like ours" (James 5:17). I know I compared the power of Elijah in that earlier chapter to Superman and Batman, but the prophet wasn't a superhero. He was human. But he "prayed earnestly that it would not rain, and it did not rain on the earth for three years and six months. Then he prayed again, and the sky poured rain and the earth produced its fruit" (vv. 17–18).

Righteousness

Elijah was an ordinary man who figured out how to get heaven to respond to earth. His example is recorded for us in 1 Kings as a way for us to understand the importance of this transaction we call prayer.

There was a challenge for the people—a drought that lasted three years (18:1; see James 5:17). So Elijah called on heaven to address the problem and fix it, and heaven responded.

Why was Elijah's prayer so effective? One reason is given by

James, who writes that the "fervent prayer of a righteous" person (v. 16 NKJV) can accomplish a whole lot. Righteousness entails being rightly aligned with God, first through the substitutionary atonement of Jesus Christ and second through the regular confession and forgiveness of sin. Jesus secured our righteousness with His death on the cross and His resurrection, but too few of us understand and fully live in light of this righteousness.

Many of us confuse righteousness with perfection. The Pharisees may have been guilty of that as well. When you confuse righteousness with perfection, your focus is drawn to what you are doing rather than who you are in Christ. This can ultimately lead to one of two things, or both: *pride,* which comes when you begin to successfully keep a number of the commandments or rules, or *shame,* which comes when you ultimately mess up.

Access and Authority

But righteousness leads to the right responses: humility and gratitude (out of an awareness for Christ's death on the cross), as well as a desire to do what is right from a heart of love for God Himself. When you and I live in a way that seeks after righteousness, based on Scripture's definition of our righteousness, it gives us greater kingdom access and authority in prayer.

We read about this access in Hebrews:

> Therefore, since we have a great high priest who has passed through the heavens, Jesus the Son of God, let us hold fast our confession. For we do not have a high priest who cannot sympathize with our weaknesses, but One who has been tempted in all things as *we are, yet* without sin. Therefore let us draw near with confidence to the throne of grace, so that we may receive mercy and find grace to help in time of need. (4:14–16)

When you are rightly aligned under God, you have the authority to approach His throne with confidence and boldness. And to expect Him to respond.

Ongoing Prayer

Elijah certainly hadn't read any of the New Testament Scriptures since they hadn't been written yet, but he understood what it meant to live a righteous life and to pray according to God's Word. Finally after three years "the word of the Lord came to Elijah . . . saying, 'Go, show yourself to Ahab, and I will send rain on the face of the earth'" (1 Kings 18:1). God had told him He would send the rain if Elijah would go show himself to Ahab. Yet Elijah still prayed, and he prayed with great fervency. That is a lesson to each one of us about how important our role in heaven-to-earth transactions really is.

Here's how the story unfolds, following the death of the false prophets at Mount Carmel:

> Elijah said to Ahab, "Go up, eat and drink; for there is the sound of the roar of a heavy shower." So Ahab went up to eat and drink. But Elijah went up to the top of Carmel; and he crouched down on the earth and put his face between his knees. (1 Kings 18:41–42)

He had just got done telling the king that a roar of a heavy shower was about to come. And instead of standing there waiting for it to come, Elijah positioned himself into a posture of prayer, remaining there while his servant looked off toward the sea to let him know if any rain clouds were on their way. God had told Elijah He would send rain. So if anyone had an excuse to not pray, it would have been Elijah.

At first we read that no rain clouds were in sight. Not a drop threatened to fall on the parched earth that had endured three years of drought.

Each time the servant came back to Elijah to report to him what he did not see, Elijah remained in his posture of prayer. He stayed crouched on Mount Carmel, seeking to draw down what God had already declared. I don't know about you, but if God already said it was going to rain, I might have become frustrated about the third or fourth time the servant came back with a "no" report. But Elijah stood his ground, or actually "crouched down on it." This is because Elijah knew the true power of prayer. The power comes in knowing what God already intends to do.

Elijah did not become frustrated. He did not sigh. He knew he had heard God clearly and that rain would be coming soon. Because of this, he was able to remain patient in his prayer through all six negative reports from his servant.

An interesting thing about Elijah's prayer on the mountain is how he did it. When we read that he crouched down, it also says he put his face between his knees (v. 42). That may not mean much to us today, but in Old Testament culture to put your face between your knees resembled the position a woman giving birth would assume when it came time to deliver. Most women in that day would crouch down, bend over, and push through the agonizing pain.

Elijah wasn't leaning up against a shade tree. Even though he knew that God said He would send rain, Elijah took the posture of pushing and laboring in his prayer. He fervently did his part in pulling out of heaven what was ready to be birthed on earth: rain. He was exercising kingdom authority through kingdom prayer.

Finally after the seventh trip to the sea, the servant returned and reported, "Behold, a cloud as small as a man's hand is coming up from the sea" (1 Kings 18:44). Rain was about to be released from the skies like a faucet turned immediately on full blast.

Elijah fervently did his part in pulling out of heaven what was ready to be birthed on earth: rain.

Remember, Elijah didn't make it rain. But he accessed the authority Who could. He partnered with God in ending a drought and bringing food, fruit, and life back to the land. What Elijah did through prayer was reach in and grab what God had already told him He would give.

Like Elijah, we are to consider our prayers as labor in God's presence when He has prompted us in an area to pray. Often the opposite occurs if we feel we found an answer in God's Word or He gave us a sense in our spirit through His Spirit that we no longer have to pray. We stop our efforts. Elijah's example is just the opposite. Elijah knew that God had declared it would rain. But he not only prayed, he prayed fervently, expectantly, and physically until he got a specific answer to his specific request and manifested God's spoken will in history. Like Jacob who wrestled with God all night until he got a response from heaven, there are times when we are to wrestle with God until He moves.

Our Personal Wait

When my youngest child, Jonathan, was struggling academically throughout elementary school, middle school, and high school, I repeatedly wrestled with God to help him overcome the limitations Attention Deficit Disorder had placed on him. I wrestled for years without seeing any real improvement at all. Yet eventually Jonathan did overcome those limitations, even graduating from college in three and a half years. He also went on to earn his master's degree from Dallas Theological Seminary.

You may not see the rain come immediately, your child overcome a challenge quickly, or, if unmarried, a mate appear suddenly after waiting for all these years, but you and I must press forward in prayer until heaven responds. Above all else, never quit. The small cloud appeared only on the seventh trip.

What God says He wants to do doesn't always happen immediately. Often He waits on our labor to pull it down. This is because He's given a certain dominion to us as His creation created in His image with the dominion mandate to "rule." Kingdom prayer is what can break through into the supernatural realm and invite heaven's response to earth.

The invisible gets pulled down through prayer.

THE POWER OF KINGDOM PRAYER

Praying For No Rain

I'll never forget a Columbia, South Carolina, crusade I participated in a number of years ago. About 25,000 people had turned out for this event, which was centered around racial reconciliation and community restoration. The numbers were equally divided between blacks and whites and this was a time in our nation when racial discord and distance was very high. I sensed the weight and magnitude of this event and that it would be the catalyst for the beginning of something powerful in that region, and possibly in our land.

But we almost didn't have that crusade.

Because of rain.

While Elijah had crouched and prayed on Mount Carmel for rain, at this gathering our leaders met to pray against it. The heavens threatened to pour down a storm at the uncovered football stadium that would no doubt cancel this event. The weather bureau had issued an alert that severe thunderstorms, possibly causing flooding and wind damage, were headed our way. They were due to arrive at about the same time we were scheduled to start.

Huddled in a room underneath the stadium were a group of organizing pastors, along with some others who had helped to set up the evening's agenda. Knowing that the rain would most likely shut down our entire evening, I asked if we could all pray.

There was quick agreement to the request and several of the pastors led off with prayer, but as they prayed I kept thinking that these sounded like what I would call *safe* prayers. You know the kind. They thanked God for His sovereignty and His power and told Him that they understood He could control the rain. They asked Him to hold it back *if He wanted to*, and thanked Him *if* He would. Then they passed the baton to the next man. And the next, and by the time it got to me—I can't say I added anything more than what had already been said. Doubt can be contagious.

Linda's Prayer

Yet shortly after I prayed, a petite woman named Linda lifted her hand. Perhaps she had gotten frustrated with the prayers from the so-called professionals—the preachers and the leaders.

Whatever the case, Linda then stood up and asked, "Do you mind if I pray?"

What else could we say, but "Go ahead."

Linda then began her prayer: "Lord, Your name is at stake. We told these people that if they would come out tonight that they would hear a word from God. We told them they would hear from You. Now, if they come and You let it rain, and You don't control the weather—then You will look bad. Because we told them that You wanted to say something important to them. So if we told them that You wanted to say something to them and You don't keep back what You can control, the weather, someone could say that Your name is no good."

And then she threw in a line that caused everyone to look at each other out of the corners of our eyes as she prayed. Linda said, "Therefore right now I command You in the Name of the Lord Jesus Christ to stop the rain for the sake of Your Name!"

With that, the preachers opened our eyes. Eyebrows went up. All we could say and think was "Um, did she really just pray that?"

Following the prayers, we all went up and sat on the platform. The sky had turned entirely black behind us. The person who had been assigned to communicate directly with the weather bureau said, "The showers are coming. They are heavy thunderstorms, and they are coming right at us."

It was time for the event to start, so the music began to play when all of a sudden massive lightning overhead surrounded everyone. People began to move around in their seats. Some even started to get up and open their umbrellas.

While umbrellas began to go up in the audience, and several people on the stage opened theirs—Linda sat there close by, motionless. I saw the man next to her offer her his umbrella. She brushed him off and I could see her mouth the words, "No, thank you." I could tell she felt she just wouldn't need it.

God's Answer

And then something happened that I had never seen before. The rain rushed toward the stadium like a wall of water. Yet when it hit the stadium, the path of the pounding rain split. Half of the rain went on one side of the stadium. The other half went on the other side. And then it literally met on the far side of the stadium. All the while, Linda sat there with a confident look on her face. The rest of the preachers and leaders on the platform just looked at each other. We looked at the rain going around the stadium, and then we looked at each other again. Then we looked at Linda. She stared straight ahead.

Now, this is not a story that someone told me. I was there. In fact, my family was there with me. Not only that but 25,000 people were there with me. All 25,000 of us saw a miracle that night—right in front of our eyes.

All because a little lady named Linda knew the power of kingdom prayer.

One woman stopped the rain from cancelling an entire crusade. Her petite frame held more power than all of us preachers combined. Simply because she was intimately connected with and invested in the power of prayer, a power that comes from accessing God's authority in faith. I'm sure you won't be surprised that many people gave their hearts to the Lord that night to receive salvation, their spirits being softened by just having witnessed a weather phenomenon like none other.

Whether you are praying for rain like Elijah, or against it—

like Linda—your fervent prayer of faith will accomplish much more than you have ever dreamed of. Prayer is a powerful tool in the heart of one who will not quit until what he or she believes God has said has come to pass.

PART 3

The Conditions for Kingdom Prayer

Making Mountains Move

All of us have traveled across bridges at some point in our lives. When you travel across a bridge, it typically means that two bodies of land have been separated by a challenge. Either there is a waterway—a lake or river—that cannot be crossed so a bridge is constructed. Or perhaps there is a valley in between two mountains or two high hills that is too big and lengthy to travel so a bridge is constructed instead. The bridge is designed to take you from where you are to where you are trying to go.

God has constructed a bridge for everyone reading this book today. It is a bridge for everyone who believes on the name of His Son, Jesus Christ. This bridge moves you from the natural to the supernatural. It allows you the freedom to reach a location that would have been impossible without the bridge. Not only that, the bridge gives you the opportunity to reach it faster than anyplace you could have gone on your own. This bridge God has given us is called faith.

So indispensable is faith to experiencing the authority of kingdom prayer that God says without it, "it is impossible to please Him" or be rewarded by Him (Heb. 11:6). And it is the link that transports you from where you are to where you are needing to go.

Faith is the only bridge God has provided for you to cross over from the natural to the supernatural. So if you choose not to use it, you won't get across. No matter how bad you want to or how much you need to cross over, without faith you will not move into the supernatural realm of kingdom prayer.

I like to define faith simply as acting like God is telling the truth. I know, I mentioned that definition in chapters 6 and 8, but I repeat it here because I want you to remember it. Faith is letting your actions reflect a belief system that what God says is true. Of course God *is* telling the truth, but our actions don't always mirror that belief. Especially when the truth God has declared has yet to manifest itself in our lives. That's why I also like to describe faith as acting like something is so even when it is not so simply because God said so in order that it might be so.

THE ROLE OF FAITH

While prayer is the bridge to communicating with God, faith is the movement you take on that bridge. Imagine that you and I were standing on a bridge that had been placed high above a river, and this bridge served as the only way across to the other side. Neither of us could argue that the bridge did not exist to fulfill its purpose. It did. In fact, we could both clearly see the other side of the bridge from where we stood. We knew it connected us to where we wanted to go. But what if I walked across the bridge and you decided to remain where you were. Would we both have put the bridge to use? No. A bridge is only as useful as you make it. And an unused bridge is a useless bridge.

God has given every believer a bridge that reaches directly into His throne room. He has given you access to both His ear and His voice through this bridge. But He will not force you to cross it. You must walk across the bridge on your own. That's the very definition of faith.

When you face trials, challenges, unmet expectations, and desires in your life, you need the supernatural intervention of God. We all need the supernatural intervention of God. How do I know that? Because I've been a pastor for over forty years and I've seen it in countless lives, as well as in my own. The natural solutions to life's issues don't do anything substantial or long-lasting at all. They may fix things momentarily, mask them, or distract you for a moment. But transformational and supernatural power comes only from God. And only one bridge gives you access to Him—prayer *in faith*.

THE ROLE OF UNBELIEF

Nothing will keep you stuck in your circumstances and your life issues quite like unbelief. Unbelief literally limits what God will do in and through your life. Unbelief puts handcuffs on an almighty Creator. We read in Matthew 13 that Jesus limited Himself in what He would do because of the unbelief of those around Him. It says, "And He did not do many miracles there because of their unbelief" (v. 58).

Unbelief is so powerful it will literally stop God's work in your life. It will keep God at a distance. In fact, unbelief will keep you stuck right where you are for the rest of your life, if you remain in it. You will never cross the bridge from the natural to the supernatural with unbelief. It's simply not possible.

How does this affect your prayers?

In every single way.

When God hears your prayers, He isn't just listening to your words. He's listening to your heart and your spirit. When what you say verbally does not align with the truth you believe internally, that inner truth trumps.

Let me give you an example. Imagine you are about to take a trip to London for a summer vacation. You pack your bags, lock your home, and depart to the airport. You pass through security, walk down the international concourse, and see a departure monitor, starting with Athens, Greece. Then you remember a friend of yours had gone there and really enjoyed it. So you decide you'd like to go to Greece instead. Looking up the gate number, you head to that plane and wait until it was time to board the flight to Greece.

When they call for the passengers to board, you get in line. When it is your turn to hand your ticket to the attendant, you tell her you want to go to Greece. Of course your ticket says London instead.

"I'm sorry," she says, "your ticket is for London. You cannot board this flight."

"I know it is," you reply. "But I want to visit Greece."

The attendant just smiles and asks you to step aside so she can help the next passenger get on board. This is because the only people allowed to board the flight to Greece are those who made the investment for a ticket. It was only those who aligned their wants *with* their actions.

It wouldn't matter one bit that you wanted to go to Greece. It wouldn't even matter that you said you were going to Greece. The only thing that would matter is what ticket you held in your hand. Because that ticket revealed what you ultimately believed.

Often we will pray eloquent prayers and make straight-forward requests but do so in opposition to what we believe in our heart. Of course, God looks at our heart. He looks at what we truly believe and answers us accordingly.

THE DISCIPLES' LACK OF FAITH

Jesus gives us insight into accessing supernatural kingdom power in our lives through this gift of kingdom prayer in an event that happened during His earthly ministry. Let's review the story first:

> When they came to the crowd, a man came up to Jesus, falling on his knees before Him and saying, "Lord, have mercy on my son, for he is a lunatic and is very ill; for he often falls into the fire and often into the water. I brought him to Your disciples, and they could not cure him." And Jesus answered and said, "You unbelieving and perverted generation, how long shall I be with you? How long shall I put up with you? Bring him here to Me." And Jesus rebuked him, and the demon came out of him, and the boy was cured at once.
>
> Then the disciples came to Jesus privately and said, "Why could we not drive it out?" And He said to them, "Because of the littleness of your faith; for truly I say to you, if you have faith the size of a mustard seed, you will say to this mountain, 'Move from here to there" and it will move; and nothing will be impossible to you.'" (Matt. 17:14–20)

The story begins with a father who has a son who is a lunatic and ill. Basically, he's mentally unstable. But he's also "very ill." The father begs for mercy because his son has reached the point of no control, throwing himself into fire or into water. Not knowing what to do for him, the father takes him to Jesus' disciples to help him in some way. But they cannot. They can't heal him even though Jesus had given them authority to heal and cast out unclean spirits.

We see this in Matthew 10 when Jesus commissioned His disciples for service. He said to them, "And as you go, preach, saying, 'The kingdom of heaven is at hand.' Heal the sick, raise the dead, cleanse the lepers, cast out demons" (vv. 7–8). Jesus had deputized His disciples to act on His behalf in order to help hurting people spiritually, physically, and circumstantially. He had given them the power to do all of these things to demonstrate kingdom authority. Yet when this father came to the disciples to heal his son, the disciples could not do it.

So the father went to Jesus instead and told Him that he had gone to the disciples, those Jesus appointed to help Him, but none could. The father had gone to the right place but received nothing. He was a disappointed dad coming to Christ and begging for mercy for a son he loved dearly. And when he did, Jesus immediately rebuked a demon within the boy, and it left the son.[1] The boy was cured at once.

But notice what Jesus said before He asked that the boy be brought to Him in order to cure him. He said, "You unbelieving and perverted generation, how long shall I be with you? How long shall I put up with you?" Jesus' frustration might have been worded like this to His disciples in our day:

"How long do I have to go through this with you?"

"How often do I have to tell you the same thing over and over?"

"How many meetings do we have to hold?"

"How many times do you have to watch me do this?"

Jesus was divinely ticked off. And rightfully so, no doubt. These were His disciples. These were the ones chosen to live intimately beside Him for so many years. These were the ones who witnessed His power, received His authority, and had been chosen to carry His legacy beyond His life. But they didn't get it. They didn't see all there was to see.

Maybe they were stuck on the physical reality standing in front of them—the boy covered in dirt, scars, and drool. Maybe they were stuck on the circumstances surrounding them— the hopelessness of throwing oneself into fire or water to bring an end to life and pain. Whatever the case, they couldn't see the spiritual truth through the physical fog.

When Jesus saw the boy, He rebuked a demon. He knew that behind the physical manifestations in this young man's life was a spiritual source that had to be dealt with.

Caught Up in What We See . . . or Do

This happens to us in our prayer lives, doesn't it? We get so focused on what we can see that we neglect to see all there is to be seen. We allow the physical, mental, and circumstantial realities dictate our direction—even in prayer. We allow them to dictate our beliefs. As a result, the situation or relationship or even ourselves remain unhealthy, stuck, and circumstantially bound because we have not learned how to do battle in the spiritual realm through faith. Kingdom prayer looks to the spiritual first.

If I have a headache, I'll drive down to the local drugstore and get some medicine for headaches. You might do the same. Or maybe you have a favorite tea or aroma to address the headache. Whatever the case, you are seeking to treat the physical with a physical solution. However, if someone who had a headache tried all of that and the headache was still there, they might go to the doctor. And if the doctor found a tumor, then the solution will need to be something else entirely. Even though the physical symptoms would be the same—a headache—the treatment would be much different. This is because the root of the problem would have been diagnosed and identified.

A lot of people today are living in a great deal of misery simply because they refuse to go to the Great Physician and discover the spiritual root of what is wrong in their lives. Rather, they are treating the symptoms. Or masking the pain. Or trying to forget that it exists. This is done through a variety of means: self-medication, alcohol or sex, and even entertaining distractions such as television, spending, eating, Internet, and social media. Yet none of those things will bring healing or move people toward living with the full kingdom authority God offers. Those activities may provide momentary pleasures or momentary relief, but when they dissipate the root issue that drove them there in the first place remains.

Of course, none of those things is wrong in itself. In moderation they may bring pleasure, entertainment, and more. But over time in our culture I have seen these practices taken to extremes. When that happens, the activities become a spiritual or emotional crutch, thus blocking the opportunity for a real cure. This prolongs the healing that is so desperately needed and which can come about quickly when placed in the supernatural hands of Jesus Christ in faith through prayer.

When Jesus told the demon to leave the boy, the boy was instantly healed. God does not promise instant healing today, but at times people struggling for months or years to overcome issues are delivered overnight. That's one supernatural response to kingdom prayer. When you cross the bridge of faith, God can come out of nowhere and change things in a moment.

He did it all the time in the Scriptures. When Jesus showed up—*bam*. He healed, provided, raised the dead, comforted, and so much more. Part of this was to help His people recognize His divine ministry and that He is the one sent by God, the Messiah (as He indirectly told John the Baptist in Luke 7:20–22). Few of us are accessing the full power of God's supernatural provision today, because we are like the disciples. They walked with Jesus, knew His teachings, and tried their best to obey Him. Yet they lacked one critical element for accessing the authority of the kingdom of heaven. They lacked faith that viewed the spiritual first.

WHAT'S MISSING?

Even the disciples recognized something was missing. That's why they motioned to Jesus after He finished healing the boy to come over and talk to them privately. "Why could we not drive it out?" they asked. In other words, "What's missing in us?"

Have you ever felt like asking Jesus the same thing? You have been trying to tackle and address personal situations but it's not working. You're reading your Bible. You're saying your prayers. You're going to church. But for some reason this religious thing doesn't seem to be working for you the same way it worked for Jesus. This kingdom power He spoke about, promised, and modeled couldn't be further from your own life experiences and realities. And you just want to say, "Hey, Jesus, why doesn't any of this work for me like it did for You?"

Jesus' answer to you, me, and all of us is the same as His answer to the disciples so many years ago. It was their littleness of faith, He told them. The reason they failed was because they failed to believe. When what you do or believe does not allow you to cross the bridge into the supernatural, it means that faith is either missing or it is too small, or it is in the wrong object. It does not mean that good intention is missing. It does not mean that knowledge is missing. It doesn't even mean that hope is missing. But it definitely means that faith is missing, or too small. Faith will determine your experience, or lack thereof, of the supernatural.

Jesus rebuked the disciples in telling them that their faith was insufficient for the problem. He didn't tell them they had no faith. He told them they had small faith. "Because of the littleness of your faith," He said. The disciples had enough faith to follow Him. They had enough faith to listen to the father's problem about his son. They had enough faith to try and fix it. But they didn't have enough faith to actually fix it.

THE SIZE OF OUR FAITH

So how small was their faith? It had to be smaller than a mustard seed, since that's the analogy Jesus used to show them how much faith they needed. We read, "For truly I say to you, if you have faith the size of a mustard seed, you will say to this mountain, 'Move from here to there,' and it will move; and nothing will be impossible to you" (Matt. 17:20). He told them that all they needed was mustard-seed faith to deal with mountain-size problems.

A Mustard Seed

How small is a mustard seed? It's about the size of the tip of your average pencil! That's small—which could make me, and you, confused about what Jesus just said. After all, He told the disciples they couldn't heal the boy because their faith was small. Yet then He gave them an example of how having very small faith can move a mountain.

But it's what's inside the mustard seed that matters most. Inside that seed, when planted, is a fifteen-foot tree. The seed itself may be tiny, but the life inside of it is huge.

What made the disciples' faith little was the lack of life inside of it. It was a life issue. The comparison was a living faith verses a lifeless faith because it did not see the spiritual. What makes faith small is the absence of spiritual life inside of it. When this void exists, it becomes what James describes as "dead faith" (James 2:23).

Our problem—for those of us who don't regularly access the authority of the kingdom through faith in prayer—is a lack of life in our faith. We come up with big plans, big dreams, expectations, and the lot but none of it will grow without a living faith. When something doesn't have life, it cannot grow. Jesus reminds us that we don't need to have much faith—the size of a mustard seed will do—but it does need to be living faith. That kind of faith can move mountains. Just like an acorn can literally crack concrete in two as it overrides a solid slab because the nature of the life inside of it is strong enough to break through. It is the nature of faith that accesses and draws down the power of the heavenly kingdom to earth.

> *What made the disciples' faith little was the lack of life inside of it. What makes faith small is the absence of spiritual life inside.*

There is another very important distinction in what Jesus said that we often overlook, outside of the make-up of a mustard seed. Let me restate what He said, with one slight revision, and see if you can catch it: "For truly I say to you, if you have faith the size of a mustard seed, you can say to this mountain, 'Move from here to there,' and it will move; and nothing will be impossible to you." Did you catch it? You might want to go back and compare that to the previous time I quoted the verse correctly and see if you can spot the revision.

Moving Mountains

The word is "can." In my revision, I used the word "can." But in Jesus' original statement, He used the word "will." When you change that statement from "can" back to "will," you have shifted the conversation. Jesus doesn't say you *might* have some luck in getting your prayers answered when you have the faith the size of a mustard seed. He says you *will* move the mountain with faith like that. You *will* tell the situation what it must do.

Mountains are obstacles. They are often used as symbols of problems in Scripture. So whatever issue is standing in your way, whether it be addiction, loneliness, debt, or poor health, when your living faith aligns with the will of God you *will* overcome that obstacle.

Now, remember what the disciples were trying to do Jesus had already commissioned them to do. That means they were acting in accordance with God's revealed will. Living faith must always be in alignment with God's truth and will. It's not a name-it, claim-it mustard seed. God is the sovereign of His kingdom and His rule is overarching. Yet far too few of us, believers equipped and charged with the commission of glorifying Him and expanding His kingdom rule on earth, fully live out the authority and power He has promised us if we were to have faith.

Can you imagine how different things might be if you learned how to embrace life with living faith?

Wouldn't it be something to speak to your mountains and see them move?

To speak to your issue and see it move?

Or, even better, to help someone else in Jesus' name. That kind of faith can change families, communities, churches, schools, ministries, businesses, countries, and the world.

Most of our problems today are a result of believers in Jesus Christ living unbelievingly. They are living, like the disciples, in a faith that they can see—a faith in religion and good works. Yet when it comes down to actually delivering something deep from a situation, they don't have the faith to do that.

That kind of faith is rooted in a relationship. It is rooted in intentionality. It is rooted in what Jesus concluded His explanation to the disciples by saying, "But this kind does not go out except by prayer and fasting."

When He speaks of "this kind" (Matt. 17:21), He's referring to a deep struggle. Remember, this particular demon invaded the boy. Such deep life issues can require a deep, living faith, at times expressed in fasting.

So what exactly is prayer and fasting, when you break it down to its core? It is relational and intentional communication with God, even to the exclusion of normal bodily wants or desires.

INFUSING YOUR FAITH WITH LIFE

Whatever that thing is that has been controlling you, dominating you, discouraging you, you're going to need to go deeper to move it along. Jesus didn't cast out the demon with a pill. He cast it out because He had already aligned Himself deeply in a living faith with a living God through both prayer and fasting. There are some things, many things in fact, that only God can handle.

The question then becomes: how do you infuse your faith with life, like the life found in the mustard seed? You do this by getting to know the One who is life. You do this by aligning your heart, mind, and spirit underneath God and thus experiencing His life in you. Yes, that means taking time from your daily routine to communicate with God regularly. After all, Paul did tell us to *pray always*. It means taking time when you wake up to align your thoughts from a human standpoint of "Oh Lord, it's morning!" to "Oh Lord, thank You for another morning." It means replacing complaining with gratitude. Releasing unforgiveness.

By doing all of these things, the truth of who you are aligns with the truth of God: showing love, kindness, gentleness, self-control, and all the things that comprise the nature of the Holy Spirit. The closer your spirit comes to His Spirit in alignment, the greater life you will have within your faith.

Faith is not just a feeling, a wish, or even a prayer. Faith is believing that the One whom you believe in is believable. Faith is the substance within the seed. The substance of things hoped for and believed.

CHAPTER 12

The Force of Fasting

Water that kept seeping into his basement left one home-owner puzzled. He would bail out the water and dry the basement, only to have the water return. So he launched a search.

He checked all the surface water connections and then the drainage tiles around the basement. Nothing wrong there. But the water returned, and he kept bailing water and drying the basement. Finally the weary man decided to call a plumber, who soon informed him that he had a leak under the house's foundation. The problem wasn't solved until the man broke up his basement floor, fixed the problem, and laid a new floor.

Like this man, we spend time trying to bail and mop our way out of the problems and issues we face, only to discover nothing much has changed. We need to break up those old floors that are hiding the real problem and lay some new foundations. The spiritual discipline of fasting, when added to prayer, provides even greater kingdom authority.

Let's start with a definition. Fasting is *the deliberate abstinence from some form of physical gratification, for a period of time, in order to achieve a greater spiritual goal.* When you fast, it doesn't have to be from food. It can be from any form of physical gratification, including television, Internet, and social media. But often fasting is focused on the denial or limiting of food, so that will be our main focus in this chapter.

Eating is one of the fundamental components of being human. We eat several times every day to obtain the nourishment and energy we need to survive. Yet every so often, something comes up that is more important than our next meal. When they're working on a major project, many professionals will have a "working lunch." They don't leave the office because their work is more important than the meal. And if it's the last minute and they're rushing to make a deadline, they will skip lunch altogether because the task at hand is more important than food.

It's not just at the office. In many homes, looking after the kids and keeping the house running is such a nonstop job that there's no time for Mom to sit down and eat. For Mom, taking care of her kids' needs and the home is more important than food, and she may not even realize that she hasn't eaten anything all day.

What we will do often without thinking because we are busy or distracted, the Lord asks us to do intentionally when He calls us to fast. The precedent and reasons for doing so are found throughout the Scriptures.

In the Bible we see God's people fast *when they are in crisis.* When they desperately needed a breakthrough in their circumstances, their emotions, their relationships, their future, or their nation, they fasted. Fasting shows God that our need for Him is greater than our need for food, or whatever item it is we choose to restrain ourselves from. Even Jesus fasted in times of need. In Matthew 4, Jesus entered the wilderness to be tested by the devil. He prepared by fasting for forty days, and the devil's first words tempted Jesus to eat (Matt. 4:3). Jesus' response was to declare that man doesn't live on bread alone, but on every word that comes from God (quoting from Deut. 8:3).

FASTING: PLACING OUR HUNGER FOR GOD ABOVE OTHER NEEDS

By fasting, you deliberately show God that you are serious about getting His attention and that you are intently listening for His voice. Skipping a meal is not necessarily fasting. Fasting is making an intentional choice to place your hunger for God above any other need.

Remember what Jesus said to the devil? We can't live on just food because we need the Word of God even more. Fasting shows God and ourselves that His Word is more important than food. When we fast, we give the Holy Spirit our full attention.

Zechariah 7:5–6 tells us that when we eat, we do it for ourselves. But the passage goes on to say that when we fast, we do it for the Lord.

We demonstrate a brokenness that shouts, "I can't do this!" The self-sufficient man or woman won't fast, but the desperate one will. The self-sufficient nation won't fast, but the desperate one will.

The truth is we cannot live the Christian life in our own strength. We can't make things happen. We can't force victory in our life simply by strategizing one. We've got to starve our flesh to feed our spirit. When our spirits are strong and our flesh is weak, huge spiritual breakthroughs explode all over. The question is not whether fasting makes a difference. The question is, "How bad do you want a difference to be made?"

A Hungry Widow Prepares to Die

To understand the importance of fasting and the role it plays in strengthening our prayers, let's stick tight to Elijah again in this chapter. Let's look at the story of the encounter between him and the widow of Zarephath, found in 1 Kings 17.

At the time this story took place, Elijah was beginning his ministry as a prophet of the Lord. Totally dependent on God, Elijah listened for God's voice and followed Him in total trust. God directed Elijah to hide out near the brook of Cherith for a time, as we saw in our chapter on commitment and calm. Yet after Elijah had been in hiding for some time, God commanded him, "Arise, go to Zarephath, which belongs to Sidon, and stay there; behold, I have commanded a widow there to provide for you" (v. 9).

Zarephath was a hot, dry village located in Phoenicia, which is modern-day Lebanon. This region was experiencing a severe drought; no rain had fallen for months. The lack of water led to failed crops, which was a devastating blow to this agricultural society. With no crops, there was no food. This would have been an especially difficult time for the widow, who had no means of income and no family to provide for her.

The widow of Zarephath and her son were truly facing a crisis: They were preparing their last meal and were expecting to starve to death (v. 12). Yet God had instructed this widow to take care of Elijah so he could continue to carry out God's kingdom agenda on earth.

Elijah approached the woman, saying, "Please get me a little water in a jar, that I may drink" (v. 10). She got him some water, and he then went on to request even more of her. This time he asked her for food. He said he wanted a piece of bread. She replied, "As the Lord your God lives, I have no bread, only a handful of flour in the bowl and a little oil in the jar; and behold, I am gathering a few sticks that I may go in and prepare for me and my son, that we may eat it and die" (v. 12).

The widow knew that Elijah was coming and that she had been commanded by God to provide for him (v. 9), but when the time came for her to obey God's instruction, she looked at her desperate circumstances and allowed the practical matter of having no food stand in the way of obeying God. Yet faith is a confidence that God is able to meet the need you bring before Him, and at this moment in time, the widow faltered in her faith: she had not prayed to God for help.

Looking Beyond Circumstances

Just like the widow of Zarephath, many of us claim we believe in God, yet we follow Him only when it's practical. We would prefer to listen to common sense rather than to call on the Lord. *How can He help in this time of famine?* But God doesn't always function in the way we call "practical." When He speaks to His people, He wants to know, "Do you have enough confidence in My Word to step out and trust Me?" The widow was saying to Elijah, "Yes, I believe in God, but in the real world, where I live, I am a destitute widow, and I have no bread to give you."

All she saw was that she had a little bit of flour and some oil. But, if you look at the situation with a different perspective, you recognize that flour and oil are the ingredients needed to make bread! The widow had what she needed to do what God told her to do, but in her eyes it wasn't practical. She let her circumstances govern her decision, and her fear overruled her faith.

Although the widow used her physical sight to view her situation, Elijah used his spiritual sight to perceive what God could do. Elijah told her, "Do not fear; go, do as you have said, but make me a little bread cake from it first and bring it out to me, and afterward you may make *one* for yourself and for your son. For thus says the Lord God of Israel, 'The bowl of flour shall not be exhausted, nor shall the jar of oil be empty, until the day that the Lord sends rain on the face of the earth'" (vv. 13–14).

Elijah saw that not only did she have enough to feed herself and her son, she could feed Elijah too! Notice that after the widow received God's Word, there was a shift in her response. Her confidence grew and she was able to take a step in faith that she had been unable to take before. She "went and did according to the word of Elijah, and she and he and her household ate for many days. The bowl of flour was not exhausted nor did the jar of oil become empty, according to the word of the Lord which He spoke through Elijah" (vv. 15–16).

When Elijah shared God's Word with the widow, she was reminded of the true nature of the Lord. This displays why we all need people to speak the Word of God in our lives—pastors, teachers, friends, family members. When we forget God's faithfulness, these people remind us that God's Word tells us He will take care of us. Their words remind us that biblical living overcomes practical living.

Stepping Out in Faith

Many of us have immediate needs that we pray about. Maybe we even pray frequently about them. But if we do not step out in faith, we limit the opportunity to see the supernatural hand of God. Satan will use our doubts to set up his corrupt authority in our lives. The best way to resist Satan's influence is to go ahead and obey the Lord in spite of our fears and doubts. Obedience knocks down the wall of doubts. Action is proof of the existence of true faith.

The widow chose to obey God despite her fear, and she prepared food for Elijah. Her act of obedience is the true definition of a fast. The widow was down to her last meal, yet she sacrificed it in order to obey God. And God blessed her obedience. Scripture tells us that God took that flour and made it just keep on coming so that Elijah, the widow, "and her household ate for *many* days" (v. 15, emphasis added). God met her needs because she operated in faith, not fear.

Friend, fear does not have to paralyze you. When you take the tiniest step in faith, you begin a walk of faith. The widow gave up something physical—her food—as an act of faith. Her obedience increased her confidence and trust in God, and He blessed her.

THE GIVING PRINCIPLE:
GIVE IT UP . . . AND RECEIVE

This simple story illustrates a bigger kingdom principle of fasting and obeying at work in God's Word. We have looked at it earlier but let's review it for good measure. "Give, and it will be given to you," Jesus said. "They will pour into your lap a good measure—pressed down, shaken together, and running over. For by your standard of measure it will be measured to you in return" (Luke 6:38).

As mentioned in chapter 6 (under "Powerful Prayers Are Giving Prayers"), the most important word in this verse is "it." What does "it" refer to? "It" is what we give. The principle is:

Give, and whatever you give will be given back to you. The widow of Zarephath needed food, and God asked her to give food to His cause. She had to be willing to act in faith in the very arena of her need.

In our lives, when we give of ourselves and our bag is emptied, God will bless us so much that He packs in the blessings until they overflow. Luke 6:38 illustrates the principle of giving with the image of grain collected into a bag. When that grain was gathered, the collector would press it down and shake it so that more grain could fit in the bag. The same principle is taught in Galatians 6:7: "Do not be deceived, God is not mocked; for whatever a man sows, this he will also reap." You will reap the very thing you plant. You don't sow pineapples and reap watermelons. You sow watermelons and reap watermelons. God will bless you in the same way you bless others; when you give to His kingdom purpose, you become a channel through which God can express Himself to someone else.

The widow of Zarephath gave up one meal, and God provided her with food to last many days. She fasted—gave up something tangible—and God gave her more blessing "pressed down, shaken together, and running over." Her fast was a sacrifice of food, one of the most basic and essential needs of the human body. She was preparing to die of starvation. She gave up a need of the flesh because she had a greater need for the Spirit.

God promises to meet your needs. His Word is full of promises that when we ask, it will be given to us. Paul writes that "God will supply all your needs according to His riches in glory" (Phil. 4:19). But such promises always link God's provision to our obedience, even sacrifice. If you are selfish with sharing God's goodness to you, He will withhold His greater goodness from you. Many of us want from God what we are not willing to give someone else. If you are not willing to be a blessing, then God is not obligated to His promises to give you blessings. They are tied to your heart's connection to His own kingdom will and agenda.

The widow of Zarephath connected with the power of God through prayer as well as faith, obedience, and fasting. She obviously believed in and communicated with God, because He told her Elijah would be coming. When Elijah encouraged her with the Word of God, she coupled her belief with action. In like manner, when you pray and then act, you too will see the hand of God.

Perhaps you have been praying for something specific for days, months, or even years, yet you have seen no answer to your prayer. I encourage you to keep on praying. Praying is like priming a pump to get water. Sometimes you have to pump for quite a while before you get any water to come out. You have to give before you receive. When you pray and fast, when you obediently sacrifice, God will give you even more than you gave up for Him. His Word promises us this.

The Bible tells another story about a widow who makes a great sacrifice in Luke 21:1–4. The widow gave her last few pennies to God as an offering. Why didn't she use those pennies to buy bread or something practical to help her survive? Because she reasoned that God could do more with those few pennies than she could. Those pennies might get her food for a day or

> *Praying is like priming a pump to get water. Sometimes you have to pump for quite a while before you get water to come out.*

two, on her own. But in relinquishing them to God, she was investing in more than a day or two. She was investing in her entire future.

Over and over again in Scripture, the principle of obedience, sacrifice, and fasting is clear. If you want something from God, give it to Him or give up the very thing you want and believe He will provide for you. When it comes back to you, it will overflow. God will do exceedingly beyond all you think or imagine (Ephesians 3:20). And in doing so, He will meet your deepest needs.

THE HEART OF FASTING

According to Isaiah 58:4, the purpose of fasting is "to make your voice heard on high." When we fast with the proper heart, our voice is heard in heaven. Fasting isn't simply something you throw into your routine. You can't just skip a meal or a television show and call it a fast. Well, you might call it a fast but God won't. The heart must accompany the action.

The nature of fasting is such that it demands concentrated effort and intentionality to come into God's presence.

Think about the effort we make to eat when we're hungry. Most of us will make a way where there is no way when it's mealtime. Why? Because we are desperate to satisfy our hunger. But when we fast, we are desperate to satisfy something much deeper—a spiritual need. We are desperate to make our voices heard on high.

The Lord says through Isaiah that fasting is "a day for a man to humble himself" (58:5). It is a humbling experience to say no to something you crave, to bow low before God and admit there is a need. Fasting demands humility, and humility means self-denial.

Sharpening Our Spiritual Focus

Something unique happens when we fast. God sharpens our spiritual focus so we can see things more clearly. Jesus fasted for forty days before facing the devil (Matt. 4:1–11). And when Satan tempted Him to make bread out of the stones, Jesus said, "Man shall not live on bread alone, but on every word that proceeds out of the mouth of God" (v. 4).

In 1 Thessalonians 5:23, Paul prayed that his readers would be sanctified and preserved in their "spirit and soul and body." Paul's order here is purposeful. We are not made up of body, soul, and spirit, but spirit, soul, and body. We are created to live from the inside out, not from the outside in. You say, "Why is that important?" Because if you look at yourself as a body that happens to house a soul and a spirit, you will live for your body first. But if you understand that you are spirit at the core of your being, you will live for the spirit.

Your spirit is the part of you that enables you to communicate with God. It gives you God-awareness. Your soul enables you to communicate with yourself. It gives you self-awareness. Your body enables you to communicate with your environment. It gives you other-awareness.

We need to live from our spirit out to our bodies. The reason so many people have messed-up bodies is because they have messed-up souls. And the reason they have messed-up souls is because their spirits are not under the control of the Holy Spirit. If we want to really live, the spirit or the inner person must be set free. Our spirits must be cracked open to release the Spirit's life, and fasting helps us do this. It enables us to make a kingdom connection.

Being Humble and Depending on Him

Far too often, our problem is that we aren't ready for God to work in our spirit. We make all kinds of resolutions and promises, which are really just ways of saying to God, "I can do this myself." But if we could do it, we would have already done it.

What God wants to hear us say is, "Lord, I can't do this. I've tried everything I know and I can't fix it. Lord, I throw my inability and my lack at Your feet."

God says, "Now I can do something."

You see, when we fail to humble ourselves before God, what we wind up doing is trying to live the Christian life in our own power. We call on our flesh to help us defeat the flesh—which is a contradiction in terms. What we need is to get the flesh out of the way, to set it aside in order to focus on the spirit. Fasting is a tangible way of demonstrating to God that we are setting aside the flesh in order to deal with the spirit.

More than that, fasting is a way of prostrating ourselves before God. In the Bible, when people were broken before the Lord they often fell on their faces. They put ashes on their heads and tore their clothes as a way of saying, "Lord, I can't do anything. I am at the end of my rope."

God wants us to reach that point so He can demonstrate His power and get all the glory, which He deserves. The apostle James says those who humble themselves before God will be lifted up (James 4:10). Fasting puts us on the path of humility.

THE PRACTICE OF FASTING

What does a person do who wants to practice fasting?

The details of a fast are really up to the individual. The

length and nature of the fast needs to be a matter of conviction between you and God. David said he put on sackcloth during a fast (Ps. 69:11). We don't usually practice the outward signs of fasting today. In fact, Jesus told us not to make it obvious to others that we are fasting (Matt. 6:16–18).

Humility and Prayer

But there are some common elements to the fasts we read about in Scripture. One is the attitude of humility before the Lord we just mentioned. Another common element in the practice of fasting is linking fasting with prayer. Listen to the prayer David offered during his fast:

> My prayer is to You, O Lord, at an acceptable time; O God, in the greatness of Your lovingkindness, answer me with Your saving truth. Deliver me from the mire and do not let me sink; may I be delivered from my foes and from the deep waters. May the flood of water not overflow me nor the deep swallow me up, nor the pit shut its mouth on me. (Ps. 69:13–15)

David came before God in humility and fasting and prayer.

God told His people through the prophet Joel, "Return to Me with all your heart, and with fasting, weeping and mourning; and rend your heart and not your garments" (Joel 2:12–13a). Fasting is a serious time of coming before God.

Praise

But it is also a time of praise. Joel went on to say, "[The Lord] is gracious and compassionate, slow to anger, abounding in lovingkindness and relenting of evil. Who knows whether He will not turn and relent and leave a blessing behind Him?"

(vv. 13b–14). Then the prophet said, "Consecrate a fast" (v. 15).

The question in fasting is, How badly do you want an answer? How much do you want deliverance? Do you want it enough to give up food or some other gratification? Then come before God with prayer and praise in fasting.

You may feel like giving up on your problems or issues, but if you haven't fasted over them yet, you haven't done everything you can do. You have one more option—to throw yourself on the mercy of God in humility while giving up a valued craving of the flesh for a greater need of the spirit.

The bottom line is when we fast, we will get God's undivided attention: "You will call, and the Lord will answer; you will cry, and He will say, 'Here I am'" (Isa. 58:9).

You may say, "But I've been calling to God all this time." Are you calling to Him with the fast? Remember, fasting makes your voice heard on high (Isa. 58:4). God wants to be treated seriously.

Be aware that once you start fasting and praying, Satan and his demons are going to line up to oppose you. They know there is power in fasting. They know fasting is like a booster rocket to your prayer, elevating you to heavenly places in order to access kingdom authority. They will want to bring you back to earth. But if you continue a fast and throw yourself on the mercy of God, He will refresh you in the heavenly places.

Through fasting God's blessings and kingdom power and authority are to be accessed. Fasting, coupled with prayer, gives you the ability to touch heaven and change earth.

CHAPTER 13

Aligning through Abiding

For most of us, the people we know better than any other on earth are those in our family. We share heartache and pleasures with them, spend the abundance of our time with them, and commit ourselves to their well-being above all others. As such, these loved ones frequently are the ones who lift us up when we are down and we love them for it.

During His time on earth, Jesus spent more time with His disciples than anyone else. They got to know His voice, thoughts, mannerisms, pet peeves, perhaps even His unique facial expressions. When He was crucified, they were devastated in ways to which few of us can relate.

So when He appeared to the two on the road to Emmaus (Luke 24:13–34), Jesus prevented them from recognizing Him at first, so He could learn their true passions and feelings about His death. But as Luke 24:29–31 points out, their eyes were opened to everything, including who He really was *when He broke the bread and gave it to them.* This action closely resembles His actions in the Lord's Supper, when He taught them and forewarned them of what was to come. In the intimate act of eating with the Master, these two disciples knew who He was and they were immediately encouraged.

When life drags you down and struggles become unbearable, your ability to rise above it all hinges on your intimate communion and abiding with Christ.

Do you spend time with Him, praying and reading His words? Just like you spend time with your family, sharing the joys and sorrows together, do you give your burdens to and share all your victories with Christ?

In short, do you live as though you are *in* Him? Do you abide? Effective kingdom prayer is entirely dependent upon your abiding relationship with Jesus Christ, as we have looked at previously. But what exactly does it mean to abide in Jesus?

TO ABIDE IN JESUS

Some Definitions

Jesus uses the word "abide" ten times in the first ten verses of John 15, as He tells the disciples to "abide in Me." So it would seem that God really wants you to know what abiding in Him is all about. We have mentioned the concept of abiding earlier, but here are a few simple definitions of *abide*: to "live or stay somewhere"; to "remain or continue"; to "wait for." One who abides in a place or with a person often will "endure without yielding."

The Presence of Fruit

Many of us say we love Jesus and abide in Jesus but there's nothing to see—no fruit. Scripture tells us that if and when we abide with Jesus, we will bear much fruit (John 15:5). If your relationship with Christ is invisible to others, there's not much of a relationship, because fruit always should be visible.

The nature of the tree will define the fruit. An orange tree produces oranges, an apple tree produces apples, and a pear tree produces pears. If we're abiding with Christ then what should be coming out of our lives that is visible ought to be God-like because our fruit takes on His nature. And just as important, if the fruit we produce is rotten, then we are not reflecting God's nature. Something's wrong. Something's off.

When Paul writes of this fruit in Colossians 1:10, he connects it with knowing God. It says, "so that you will walk in a manner worthy of the Lord, to please Him in all respects, bearing fruit in every good work and increasing in the knowledge of God."

The word "knowledge" translated in the Greek is *epignosis*, which means full knowledge or experiential knowledge. It's not information knowledge alone. Epignosis doesn't mean you have memorized some Bible verses or you've read your Bible. Rather, epignosis has to do with entering into an experience. There is an intimacy and experiential connection with God that produces fruit. In fact, it *must* produce fruit to truly be a connection with God.

The problem is that so many of us as Christians want to go to heaven but we don't care about being fruitful here on earth. But what God wants is that our experience with Him will give birth to some luscious fruit—the fruit of character and conduct that contributes to and benefits others. The fruit of faith-filled kingdom prayers grow out of a kingdom relationship.

So important is the subject of fruit that virtually a whole chapter in the Bible is given to the discussion. If we look more deeply at John 15, we will see the pattern. Verse 1 reads, "I am the true vine, and My Father is the vinedresser." Jesus is the "true vine." Anything else is a cheap imitation. Then He goes on to say that God is "the vinedresser." A vinedresser takes care of the vine, making it most productive.

In verse 2, Jesus refers to "every branch in Me." Who is "every branch"? That refers to Christians—you and me. We are the branches Jesus is talking about. So, there's a vine (Jesus), tended by the vinedresser (God), and there are branches growing from the vine (that's every person who has trusted Jesus Christ for the forgiveness of their sins and received the gift of eternal life—you and me).

Concerning the branches, Jesus explains, "Every branch in Me that *does not bear* fruit, He takes away. And every branch that bears fruit, He prunes it so it may bear *more* fruit" (v. 2, emphasis added). God "takes away," or cuts out, those branches that do not bear fruit because they are dead. But He doesn't just let the branches that are alive grow as they want to. Instead, He prunes them so the branches will bear more fruit.

In verse 5, Jesus adds that "he who abides in Me and I in him, he bears *much* fruit" (emphasis added). Verse 16 tells us that Jesus appointed us to go and bear fruit, and that our fruit would *remain*. So this fruit that Jesus speaks of must be very important. If we don't produce this fruit, we are cut off. But when God prunes us, we bear *more* fruit. And when we abide in Christ, we bear *much* fruit. And as we continue to abide in Christ, He appoints us to go, telling us that our fruit is to *remain*. This fruit is getting bigger and better as we go along.

God says, "I want to move you from no fruit to fruit, to more fruit, to much fruit." You say, "Yes, God, but how do I get that? I want fruit that's rich and vibrant, exciting and meaningful."

I can distill this down to one word. If you understand this one word and act on this one word, you will begin to experience God like never before, and you will experience your prayer life explode like never before. So what's this word? It's *abide. We are to remain or continue with Jesus*

If we think about John 15 again, who is to do the abiding? It's the job of the branch to abide on the vine so nutrients will flow into the branch and produce the fruit. And we've already learned that *we* are the branches, connected to the vine (Jesus) and tended by the vinedresser (God).

Here's a picture of what it means to abide: When a woman carries her unborn child, the umbilical cord connects the baby with the mother. The baby receives needed nutrients from her mother. Mom eats and the baby is nourished. As the baby abides in her mother, she grows. Now if there was a breach in the connection between mother and baby, what would happen? Well, that baby would no longer be able to get needed nutrients and could not grow. In the case of the baby, abiding is absolutely necessary for continued growth and maturity.

Staying Connected throughout the Day

What about Jesus? Are you abiding in Him? Let's say you are faithful to attend church every Sunday. You go to church knowing that you'll sing about Jesus and hear about Christ in the sermon. You may refer to your Bible to help you understand the pastor's message. For two hours on Sunday it's you and Jesus. But then the benediction is given and you leave church. Date's over! Oh, you may pop in for a quick visit on Wednesday evening, but you're not abiding with God; you're only visiting with Him.

Just like the baby in his mother's womb, you need to be connected to Christ every moment if you want to continue to grow and be healthy. What would happen to a baby in the womb if he or she decided to only abide every once in a while?

Jesus doesn't want us to disconnect from Him. He doesn't want us to just give Him time (even though it's a good time) on Sunday mornings, with maybe a quick visit on Wednesday and a few minutes when we wake up each day. Instead, He wants us to abide with Him all day long, every day. Now some of this integration will be formal. We'll actually get on our knees and pray, or we'll actually sit down and read the Bible. But some of our time with God the Father and God the Son will be informal. God wants us to bring Him into the conversation—while we walk and while we drive, while we talk and while we are thinking.

He wants us to ask, "God, what do you think about this before I make a decision?" He wants us to ask Him to help us on the small things as well as the large. He wants to guide your thoughts so you will even know what to pray. He wants to hear from you all of the time and you do that by engaging God in prayer regularly.

"So whether you eat or drink or whatever you do, do it all for the glory of God" (1 Cor. 10:31 NIV). Bring God to bear on everything in your life. Stay plugged in. Lots of people just want a microwave experience with God, but God wants us to have a Crock-Pot experience instead. This attitude explains a lot of our problems and defeats.

With the microwave experience, you push the worship button—bam! "I've got this many minutes, God, so set me on fire." At church we get excited and we shout and we're happy and it feels like God is all over the place! But we all know something about microwaved food. It gets hot real quick, but it'll get real cold real quick as well. So you may leave church hot on Sunday morning but you're cold by the time you hit your car in the parking lot or open the door to your home when you get back. And you know you're cold because you're not talking out there like you were talking inside the building. That's a microwave experience.

God is interested in a Crock-Pot experience. Now a Crock-Pot is slow. You can leave a slow cooker on all day or all night long and when you come back to it, the food is cooked through and it's hot. You can serve that food and it'll still be hot when you take the last bite. That's what God wants for you—an ongoing experience in a rich environment that doesn't become cold and disconnected. Kingdom prayer is intensified when it is connected to a kingdom relationship.

ABIDE MEANS TO MEDITATE

Another word for abide is "meditate." We need to keep meditating on the things of God until they take root and become a part of us. The idea is to get that Word into your heart so you can begin to transform. Suddenly you realize that you're changing. You realize that you're not talking like you used to talk; not acting like you used to act; not wanting the stuff you used to want. You've changed. Your prayers have changed. You are seeing answers. And the reason is simple—you've been hanging out with God. That is abiding. And that takes time.

The Tea Dippers and the Tea Abiders

Here's a great illustration to show what abiding looks like.

There are two kinds of tea drinkers: there are the dippers and then there are the abiders. Dippers take the tea bag and put it in their cup of hot water. Then they grab the string on the tea bag and go down and up, down and up. Now if you're a dipper, that's a lot of work. You have to dip down and then lift up; dip down and lift up; over and over again. And when the tea is how you want it, you get a spoon and set it under the tea bag and wrap the string around the spoon. Then you have to squeeze to get all the tea out of the bag before you can begin to drink.

But there's another kind of tea drinker. This person sets the tea bag in the cup of hot water and just lets it sit there, abiding in the water. No work involved. I'm a tea abider. One day I was drinking tea with a friend who happened to be a dipper. He watched me set the bag into my water and begin drinking and he said, "Oh, I could never do it that way." I asked him why and he said, "If I just let the tea bag stay in the water, my tea would get too strong."

A lot of us are like the tea bag dippers. We dip in on Sunday morning and then we lift back out. We may dip back in on Wednesday but we lift out again. We may even dip in in the morning and give God a verse or a prayer, but out we go again. We've got weak tea. But God is saying, "I want us to hang out together all the time, every single day. I want to be your running buddy. I want to be included in all your decisions. I want you to think thoughts about Me all day long. Why not tell Me thank You for your car as you drive in it? Why not let Me know you appreciate the clothes you have on today? Why not ask Me where the car keys are, or whether you should play a game with your kids right now or mow the yard? Why not involve Me in all of your life? I want to be consumed by you and then you can watch what I produce in your life, your attitude, your mindset, and your patterns."

Taking Time to Align

Paul's desire was that Christians might "be filled with the knowledge of His will in all spiritual wisdom and understanding" (Col. 1:9). Having the knowledge of God's will in all spiritual wisdom and understanding will allow you to pray according to God's will. Your desires will align with God's will. And that comes through abiding with God, spending time in prayer and Scripture to hear His voice. Answered and effective prayer is all about alignment.

Just as a car must be in alignment to move smoothly down the roads of life, we also need to be spiritually aligned with God in order to move ahead in our prayers. Doors remain closed when we are out of alignment. Alignment is one of those critical spiritual components that so many people seem to fail to grasp, and even more fail to apply. Yet it can open up your pathway to answered prayer faster than nearly anything else (John 15:5).

When a car's tires are out of alignment, you can find your car wanting to pull left or pull right. The misaligned tires can cause your hands to ache as you try to hold the steering wheel steady. A different problem will happen inside your garage when the left and right sensors of your automatic garage door fall out of alignment. If either is slightly out of line, they won't connect with the other, and the broken beam, thinking some object is in the path, will deactivate your garage door, stopping it in its path. And you won't be able to get out of the garage. But once you get both sides to align the beam of light, the "broken" door is fixed.

Once things are in alignment, everything proceeds fine. The same holds true with kingdom prayer. Jesus didn't have to beg, plead, jump up and down, sing songs, or do anything huge at all to raise a man from the dead. He just said, "Lazarus, come forth." Likewise, when He divided up a couple loaves of bread and some fish to feed thousands of people, He didn't agonize in His prayer. He was in alignment with God's plan and that was enough, and then He started the process of passing out lunch.

Answered prayer can be a simple process when you are in alignment with God. As Christ said, "If you abide in Me, and My words abide in you, ask whatever you wish, and it will be done for you" (John 15:7). You really can't get any more straightforward and clear than that. Simply abide in Christ and allow His words to abide in you, and then whatever you pray will come about.

So if you want to discover the power of answered prayer, it comes through this process called abiding in Christ and His words. It comes through the process of aligning your thoughts, beliefs, and desires in cadence with His.

EXPECTING MIRACLES

The Red Sea parted, the thousands fed, the dead raised—it is awe-inspiring to recount God's miracles. Are you, as I am, fascinated with these sensational stories about God's power? Miracles get our attention because we desire to see miracles in our own lives. Miracles give us hope that God can do the undoable!

Right now, I imagine you could think of one, two or even twenty miracles you would love to see happen in your life. We all can. What if, in the blink of an eye, God took away that chronic pain, erased that heavy debt, mended that broken relationship, or dropped that dream job right in your lap?

God is powerful enough to do just that. He has the resources. He has the wisdom. He is able. And He loves us. Why, then, doesn't He go ahead and do the miraculous all the time?

I'll tell you why: The God of the Red Sea, of the loaves and fishes, of the grave, and of every problem in your life and mine, intervenes with His power when it is according to His will and for His overarching kingdom purpose. If you want to see a miracle, you are going to have to align your heart with His. After all, God is not a vending machine. We can't insert our prayers, press the button, and receive a miracle. Nor is He a body builder, flexing His miracle muscles to impress the ogling crowd. Neither is God a bottle of aspirin, medicating our aches and pains.

Remember this when you go to pray: God is as purposeful as He is powerful. Behind every miracle lies a greater plan. Unfortunately, most of the time, our reasons for wanting miracles do not match up with His reasons for doing them. Remember Mary, the mother of Jesus, and how she wanted Jesus to turn the water into wine? Ultimately, Jesus did the miracle, but He did it in such a way so as to not draw undue attention to Himself. Jesus' mother was ready for her one-of-a-kind Son to be on display, but He was not. Just like our reasons and rationale are not always the same as God's. We view things from our finite perspective when God views things from a limitless, all-knowing kingdom perspective. There is a huge difference between the two.

The Gospel of John is unique among the four Gospels in the New Testament. Matthew, Mark, and Luke tell many of the same stories and teachings about Jesus. But John takes a very different approach when recounting Jesus' life and ministry. At the very end of the book, John explains his purpose for including in it what he did. It reads,

> Therefore many other signs Jesus also performed in the presence of the disciples, which are not written in this book; but these have

been written so that you may believe that Jesus is the Christ, the Son of God; and that believing you may have life in His name. (John 20:30–31)

The reason John told specific stories and accounts about Christ was to stir up belief in the hearts of the readers. In John's book, he included seven miracles of Jesus:

(1) changing water to wine (2:1–11);

(2) healing the noble man's son (4:46–53);

(3) healing the man at the Pool of Bethesda (5:1–9);

(4) feeding the 5,000 (6:4–13);

(5) walking on water (6:16–21);

(6) healing the blind man (9:1–12); and

(7) raising the dead (11:30–44).

According to John, each miracle had a specific purpose. Jesus didn't feed the crowds just because they were hungry. Jesus didn't heal the blind man just because he couldn't see. Jesus didn't walk on water just because it was in His way. Every time Jesus did something amazing and awe-inspiring, He had a deeper agenda. He always had a God-sized kingdom purpose when He did the supernatural.

Now let's look at our own situations that we pray about within this perspective. It's easy to think that money would solve our problems. A better job, a more loving husband, a more supportive wife, a cure for sickness . . . the list could go on. But lack, pain, and suffering are often just symptoms of much deeper problems. Have you ever known someone to come into some money that gets them out of debt but in less than a year, they are facing money problems all over again? Maybe you are that person. Or a couple who is able to resolve a difference but in less than a day, there's another one vying for their attention.

Life's problems are most often just symptoms of something much deeper. Your debt is not the problem. Your boss is not the problem. Your spouse is not the problem. Your illness is not the problem. The miracle God wants to do in your life is often much bigger than a check, a person, or a pill.

When He comes through for you with His power, His miraculous work

> *God's miracles are reserved for His grander purposes, but they also go deeper than quick fixes.*

will fix so much more than your broken car or disrespectful child. By the time His miracle is completed, the symptoms of your problem will no longer be an issue. You will be busy celebrating the transformation God has worked in your life. This is because God seeks to transform, not just manage. Because if He were to restore only a situation, the root cause of the situation would quickly manifest new issues related to it that He would need to restore time and time again.

Not only are God's miracles reserved for His grander purposes, they also go deeper than quick fixes.

SUBMITTING TO HIS GRAND PURPOSES

Submit Always

The only way to see God do the impossible in our lives is first to submit to seeing those grander purposes accomplished, no matter what they are. We do this by aligning our hearts and desires with His own. We do this by praying according to His will.

For example, maybe you are praying for a new job and you have your eye on a particular location. But rather than continuing to pray for this particular job at this particular location, ask God to give it to you if it is His will but ask Him ultimately to align your heart with where He would have you.

One way to pray this is by saying, "Lord, I ask for this (particular thing). Please allow it, or something greater according to Your higher purposes, to come about." When you do this, you open the door for God to align your mindset with His own and you also give Him permission and freedom to address the root cause that has caused whatever you are praying about to occur or show up as a desire in your life. This is the kingdom perspective in our approach to prayer.

Submit Even During the Hard Times

Have you ever wondered why God allows you to go through hard times?

Have you ever asked Him why He doesn't step in and do what you know He can do?

Have you ever been angry with Him for not taking better care of you?

If the answer to any of those questions is "yes," then know that God can do something about those hard times but He will often wait until your heart, mind, and spirit are in alignment with His plans. Check your prayer list and then examine your heart. Are you begging for an aspirin and refusing to allow God to give you an X-ray? What are you holding back from Him? Are you asking Him for a specific man or woman to marry rather than the one He may have chosen for you? Are you ready for Him to accomplish His full and complete purposes in your life, or will you only be satisfied if He does what you want?

Struggles and strife are impossible to avoid. I've never met a human being who lived without them. It's natural for us to turn to our powerful, capable, heavenly Father in prayer when life gets too hard to bear. Yet before you get disappointed in how He responds to your prayers, you need to understand His character, purposes, and will. Yes, God can always come through. A miracle waits for you, though it may not look like what you were expecting. Pray for miracles. Expect them. But just know that the pathway to the supernatural always involves abiding in Christ and His words to such a degree that your heart beats in cadence with His own.

God-sized miracles never just treat the symptoms; they transform the entire person. In the midst of your hard time or unanswered prayers, consider afresh what kind of miracle you are waiting for God to do. Ask yourself if your purpose matches His and do your expectations align with His. Do your desires reflect His? When the answers to those questions is "yes," your kingdom prayers will accomplish much (James 5:16).

CHAPTER 14

The Purity of Purpose

Each of us has a spare tire in our car. The extra tire is there just in case the regular tire develops a flat or a slow leak. Most of the time, we don't even think about that spare tire. But when something does go wrong, we stop the car, walk to the trunk, grab the spare tire, and get out of a bad situation.

For most of us, prayer is like that spare tire. It's there just in case. Prayer is easy to forget about it until we really need to get out of a jam. Many of us have given up on prayer because while it is something we are supposed to do, it just doesn't seem to work. Nothing happens. Or, at least, nothing happens right away or in a way that we want it to happen. And so we kick our beliefs like we kick the flat tire in frustration. And we walk away from prayer, just as sometimes we can't change the tire and decide to call someone to replace the flat.

Yet kingdom prayer is not some sort of casual, mundane exercise you throw in before you eat or when something goes wrong. It is a mechanism created by God designed to proactively bring heavenly involvement into a historical context.

KINGDOM PRAYER:
ACCESS TO THE RULER

His Will, Our Plans

Kingdom prayer is the passport to access a foreign land and the Ruler of that land. It is our access to all God has in store for us. As the apostle John wrote, "This is the confidence which we have before Him, that, if we ask anything according to His will, He hears us. And if we know that He hears us in whatever we ask, we know that we have the requests which we have asked from Him" (1 John 5:14–15).

All you ask for will be granted—based on one contingency and it is found in this verse. It says: "If we ask anything according to His will, He hears us." God tells us that when we ask "according to His will," He hears us. We are not to name and claim just anything that comes to mind. We are to seek that which God Himself desires for us. We are to pray for that which is in alignment with His will. Every single prayer or request you make in accordance with His will comes about in history. But far too few pray with that insight or with that level of surrender.

Keep in mind, to pray according to God's will means to give up your own plans.

The disciples gave Jesus a very revealing request one day. They asked Him to teach them how to pray. Their request is significant. They did not ask Him to teach them to preach, even though He was the greatest preacher who ever lived. Neither did they ask Him to teach them to teach, even though they were with the greatest teacher of their day. They didn't even ask Him to teach them to heal. So why did they ask Jesus to teach them to pray? Most likely because they saw that when Jesus prayed, He was never turned down. Every single time He asked something from the Father, He got a positive answer. They witnessed kingdom authority in His prayers.

The disciples saw prayer in a way we rarely do—as a mechanism of exchange between heaven and earth. They observed a communion of intimate connection between the physical and the spiritual. If we were to come to view prayer in the manner that Christ carried it out while on earth, our prayer lives would be the most important aspect of who we are—rather than an afterthought.

Christ tells us this multiple times in Scripture:

"Whatever you ask in My name, that will I do, so that the Father may be glorified in the Son." (John 14:13)

"You did not choose Me but I chose you, and appointed you that you would go and bear fruit, and *that* your fruit would remain, so that whatever you ask of the Father in My name He may give to you." (John 15:16)

"In that day you will not question Me about anything. Truly, truly, I say to you, if you ask the Father for anything in My name, He will give it to you." (John 16:23)

Did you catch the repeated phrase in each statement of Christ? He tells us one of the secrets to answered prayer and that is asking in His name. If we want to get a response from the Father, we should ask in the name of the Son.

The Authority of Jesus' Name

So what's in a name? Both in Bible times and today a name represents the identity and authority of the person behind the name. In order to use the name correctly, you must use it legitimately. For example, when someone issues a "power of attorney," he or she is giving someone else the right to use their name. That means whatever authority their name carries, the power of attorney now has the same exact authority in making decisions or bringing things about.

Jesus' death, burial, and resurrection gave each of those who trust in His name for salvation the right to use that name as a power of attorney, the same way He did with the Father. Which means that anything that is aligned with God's will shall be granted in Jesus' name. Anything. Even the seemingly impossible.

Take a look at what happened when Lazarus had died. We already talked about this passage in another chapter but for the sake of the principle in it with regard to Jesus' name—let's look at it again here.

Martha (Lazarus's sister and a friend of Jesus) met Jesus on His walk to their home and burial grounds. She told Jesus that Lazarus was dead. Jesus responded that he was only asleep but Martha wouldn't accept that because she had seen him die. She had helped prepare his body for the grave. She told Jesus He was wrong; Lazarus was dead.

Seeing that she wasn't grasping where He was going in the conversation, Jesus took another approach by telling Martha Lazarus would rise again. Yet she still didn't comprehend and explained that she understood he would rise again on the last day when all are resurrected.

Jesus' Authority over Death

That's when Jesus revealed something He was not in the habit of revealing, something deep about His own character and power. He told Martha, "I am the resurrection and the life; he who believes in Me will live even if he dies" (John 11:25).

Martha may have known her Bible. She may have known her theology. But she wasn't yet acquainted with this aspect of Christ. He told her He is *the* resurrection. He has authority over death.

That changed everything.

When you discover who Jesus is, it changes how you thought things were. The same is true for you. You may be looking at whatever issue you are facing right now and be thinking that this thing is dead. Perhaps it's a marriage relationship or a dream of a certain career. Maybe it's a friendship, finances, health, or even your hope. Whatever it is, when you come to know the substance of the One to whom you pray—that He Himself is the resurrection of all things dead, you will pray differently. You will pray in faith. You will pray in expectation that God can turn it around. Knowing His name changes the nature of things. It changes the outlook on things. It changes how you pray.

Let me put it this way. Jesus' name grants you legal authority to do business in heaven on behalf of earth. His name gives you legal authority. Kingdom prayer is that point of connection between accessing the rights Christ has secured for you in heaven and bringing them to bear in your life on earth.

In your home and mine electricity is an invisible power that gives us visible privileges. It turns the lights on, makes the toaster work, heats up the oven, and more. But none of those things works on its own. Not one will work only by pushing a

> *Knowing His name changes the nature of things, the outlook on things, and how you pray.*

plug into the socket. Each can work when you flip the switch. Turn the switch and you access the electricity. You must make a connection before you can gain the power.

Every believer in Christ has things that can work in our lives to give us greater power, productivity, peace, comfort, joy, and more. You have those things as well. But you have to flip the switch. Prayer is your switch that accesses the authority of Jesus' name. Prayer in Christ's name turns on the power so that you can see God's hand show up in your life, to move things and do things that are not possible without Him.

ACCESS DENIED: PRAYERS ASKED OUTSIDE GOD'S WILL

With this being true, why then are so many of our prayers unanswered? Because we are not asking for what God is asking for. We are not asking for His will. Not only are we not asking for it, often we don't even recognize it or want it. This is because we are too tied to our own wants and worldly wisdom to surrender to God's will. God promises to give you and me everything we ask according to His will. So the key to answered prayer is aligning your requests with God's will.

Sources of God's Will: The Bible

That leads us to the next question: where do you find out what God's will is? You will discover God's will in two places. First of all, God has placed His revealed will for us in plain sight—in the Bible. The Bible is the expressed will of God in written form. It tells you what God wants, from a universal standpoint. God will never contradict in your life what He wrote in His Word. What has been written is settled in heaven. It's eternal truth. Therefore you should always start framing your mindset and requests based upon the wisdom of the Word of God. A kingdom mindset must inform kingdom prayer.

Far too many Christians are praying for things that God's revealed will has already made clear He is not going to give. When that is the case, it doesn't matter how long you pray, fast, or wait—the prayer won't access what you want it to. Remember, effective prayer will tap into the will of God. If what you are praying for and seeking goes against God's revealed will, He is not going to contradict His Word, values, character, and truth to give it to you.

Sources of God's Will: The Holy Spirit

God tells us a lot about His will in His Word. But He doesn't tell us specific things such as should you take the job with IBM or Xerox. He doesn't tell you if you should date Joe or James. None of those sorts of things are in the Bible. There are times in our everyday lives when God's revealed will in Scripture doesn't cover the specifics that we need to make a decision or to pray according to His will. That's where the role of the Holy Spirit comes into play. The Holy Spirit is there to be a witness to the written Word in your daily life. His job is to apply it to your circumstances. That might be different than how He applies it to someone else's circumstances. The Holy Spirit's role is to give you discernment on how to integrate the truth of God's Word into your daily choices.

He's kind of like a highlighter. You know how you use a highlighter when you are reading something that jumps out to you and you don't want to ever forget it. You go over the words with a colored marker so that at some point in the future you can access them easily and be reminded of their truth. The Holy Spirit acts a highlighter to apply the Word of God to your daily situations. How does He do that? He does it through your relationship with Him.

Unfortunately our relationship with the Holy Spirit is often one of the most underutilized aspects of the Godhead. And yet it is the Holy Spirit who is our guide, teacher, director, and so much more. The Holy Spirit opens the eyes of our heart, soul, mind, and spirit to see what God is doing, thinking, desiring, and pursuing on our behalf. The Holy Spirit personalizes God's revealed will into the minutiae of our lives.

Time with the Father

As noted in earlier chapters, Jesus spent much time with His Father. Jesus refers to this closeness to the Father in His healing of the paralytic sitting beside the healing pool of Bethesda. At the end of their conversation, Jesus tells him to pick up his mat and walk. After being paralyzed for thirty-eight years, the man does just that. But because the healing happens on the Sabbath, the watching Pharisees criticize Jesus. His answer is very revealing: "Truly, truly, I say to you, the Son can do nothing of Himself, unless it is something He sees the Father doing; for whatever the Father does, these things the Son also does in like manner. For the Father loves the Son, and shows Him all things that He Himself is doing" (John 5:19–20).

Jesus offered an incredible insight on prayer and intimacy with God in His answer. He let the Jews know, as well as all who read this story in Scripture, that He healed the man because He saw the Father doing that in like manner. In other words, in Christ's time with the Father—whether it was in the middle of the night, when He woke up, or as He walked along the road—in His abiding time with God, He saw what God was doing. Jesus manifested in history what He saw the Father doing in eternity.

Prayer is tapping into the heart and Spirit of God Himself to see where He is working, what He is doing, what He is chasing and pursuing. The more we know the will of God, the more our prayers will be offered in alignment with it. And the more we will see them answered. Immediately.

Kingdom prayer is not supposed to be sitting down to ask God to bless everyone on your list, as well as your job. That's nice and you can say that in a few minutes, but that's not the essence of prayer. The essence of kingdom prayer is positioning yourself in the presence of God in order for God to show you what He is doing so you can access it on earth.

What Jesus revealed at the pool of Bethesda is that His time spent with God earlier in the day and the weeks before allowed for this miracle to take place in a moment. He would spend an hour with God so that He only needed a minute to impact people. Far too many of us spend a minute with God and then years with people, making little to no impact. This is because we never stop long enough to discover what God is doing. We just live by trial and error—mostly error. And wasted time.

My friend Henry Blackaby, author of the powerful book *Experiencing God,* is a great example of someone spending time with God to learn His plans. One time I asked him what his secret was. Phenomenal things seem to be a normal occurrence in this man's life, and I wondered why that happened so often for him. Henry told me it's really not that complicated. "I get up at four in the morning and spend three hours of uninterrupted time with God." Either he reads His Word, thinks about Him, praises Him—or just remains in His presence. In doing this, he gives the Holy Spirit space to intersect God's divine thoughts with his human mind.

God Speaking Directly through the Scriptures

Too many of us have wasted twenty years of our lives because we have never taken fifteen minutes a day, or an hour, to stop and listen and seek God and what He is doing. We say our prayers but our prayers are based on nothing more than whims and wishes. Whims and wishes can add up to a wasted life when they are not rooted in the substance of God's divine intentions. Jesus did the will of the Father based on the revealed will as well as on what He saw the Father doing during His time spent with Him.

Normally, you will always have both ways confirming God's will for you. His Word guides and directs while His Spirit specifies what He is doing with and through you. And sometimes God lifts certain Scripture off the page to use it as a *rhema* word for you at that moment. A rhema word is when God's Spirit speaks directly to you. His written Word is called the *logos*, it is the truth of God in print. But when the Holy Spirit guides you specifically with Scripture, applying it to your life situations, it becomes a rhema word.

KINGDOM PRAYER AND THE WAITING GAME

Friend, your whole life can be transformed by kingdom prayer. Prayer in Christ's name according to the will of God will always be answered. It will always produce results. Now, the results might not be immediate but they will come. This is one thing that trips up a lot of us. The waiting game. You know that you are saved and will one day go to heaven, but it's a timeline issue for when that will take place. You are not going to heaven now—even though that truth is a reality.

Indeed, prayer may involve the waiting game. Often God will confirm and affirm His answer to your prayer in a way that you truly believe it will come about, yet you won't know when it will come about. This is because there is a gap between the answer and the provision. There is almost always a gap. The reason is your need for preparation. God is preparing you for your answer or He is preparing the answer for you—or both. He's getting ready to make the fulfillment of a connection but it always requires the right timing.

Even though God told Abraham He was going to give him a son, there was a gap before the son came. And even though God told the nation of Israel He would take them to the Promised Land, a large gap of time occurred. And don't forget Joseph. God showed Joseph through a dream that his brothers would bow down to him. But it took almost two decades for that to take place. In each of these examples, and many more throughout the Bible, the principles actually interfered with and delayed God's timing. Abraham and Sarah tried to bring a promised son through Hagar instead of letting God open Sarah's womb, and they were delayed fourteen years before Abraham received his promised son, Isaac, by Sarah (Gen. 16:16; 21:5). Israel's trip into the Promised Land should have taken only a few days, but it wound up taking forty years because they wouldn't let God prepare them for the answer God had promised them.

I was talking with a single woman one time who told me that she knew God had a husband for her. With a convincing look in her eyes, she said "Pastor, I know that I know. God has confirmed it for me."

So I asked her, "What preparations are you making so when your mate comes you will be ready as a godly wife?" She looked back at me with a blank stare. That thought hadn't crossed her mind. But, honestly, it is a thought that doesn't cross many of our minds as we pray. Rather, we just expect to get our prayers answered with no regard to our part of the process of being ready for that time to come. Far too many of us delay the answers to our prayers because we fail to connect the intersections of answered prayer with completed preparation. That job you may be praying for—if you got it before you were ready to handle it, you may lose it or fail to maximize it. Same thing with the mate. Or perhaps God is preparing the other person or situations to be ready for you. Always remember that God has a purpose to answered prayer. God does not obligate Himself to anything other than Himself and His purposes.

Knowing this is true, it is critical to recognize that our thoughts, patience, and development need to align with God's purposes regarding our prayers. If there is a delay, seek the Lord as to why the delay may be occurring. Maybe there is an area of your life you need to deal with first. If you are a single person waiting on a mate, perhaps God wants to teach you personal responsibility first. Or maybe He wants you to get your finances right first or any number of things. The answer to your prayer doesn't always have to directly deal with the answer to *your* prayer or to *your* situation. Many times it has to do with all parties and situations involved being prepared for that answer. Allow your prayers to guide you in such a way that you grow and mature in your development—spiritually, emotionally, and physically.

When you wait patiently, you will begin to see things lining up as God connects His kingdom purpose with your kingdom prayers.

CHAPTER 15

Grace and Gratitude

G oing through college and seminary when you're married with children can take its toll on anyone's finances. Our family is no different. For years, my wife Lois performed miracles with our money to make it stretch enough to put food on the table and clothes on our kids. But one morning in particular as Lois and I shared breakfast, she looked very discouraged.

"Tony, I just can't do this anymore," she said. "It's too hard."

We talked through the strain that living on such a limited budget with four kids was putting on her. I knew she wanted to support me and believed in God's call on my life, but I could see that she'd reached a point where the burden was too heavy.

I was also convinced of my call and believed God would provide when He asked me to do something. To hear my wife tell me she couldn't go on like this was confusing; it made me wonder how God could let things get to this point. Hadn't He said He would supply?

So I decided that, knowing my primary responsibility under God as a man was to meet the emotional, physical, and spiritual needs of my family first, I would drop out of seminary and get a full-time job. I told Lois of my plan.

Then I asked her one thing: What would she need to receive today in order to support my continuing in seminary and not dropping out? I asked for a number, a specific amount.

She thought about it a while. Finally she said, "$500."

Keep in mind that this was the 1970s, when $500 was a lot of money. Unless we got $500 that very day, I would have to drop out of seminary.

So guess what I did? You better believe it: I prayed.

I believed God had called me to prepare for the ministry, and that He'd led me to this seminary. I was convinced I should stay. But He'd also called me to be a husband who was to take care of his wife. Lois said she needed $500 that day to feel equipped to support me in staying.

Prayer was all I had at that point. So prayer is what I did.

MY LAST DAY OF CLASSES?

Making my way to the seminary campus for what looked like my last day of classes, I decided not to tell anyone about my conversation with Lois. I had told God. I had prayed. That was going to have to be enough.

After attending classes, I went to the mailroom to get my mail from my box. When I opened it up, I saw something that looked like money.

There, inside my box, were five $100 bills attached to a note from a stranger. I knew nothing about him, but apparently he knew about me. He wrote that God had told him to give this to me today.

It was exactly the amount Lois had told me she needed—

and the amount I had asked God to provide. It was a literal illustration of what Jesus had taught us to pray in the Lord's prayer, "Give us this day our daily bread" (Matt. 6:11). That day the "daily bread" was $500. And God provided exactly that. I hadn't gone around looking for the money or even asking people—I only asked God. And God supplied.

THE RIGHT SOURCE OF OUR PROVISION

One reason we are to ask our heavenly Father for our food and our daily needs is that we don't want the wrong person feeding us. Did you know that the devil has a food program? He does, and he offered it to Jesus in the wilderness temptation (Matt. 4:3) just before Jesus gave the Sermon on the Mount.

Satan tempted Jesus to turn stones into bread, but Jesus refused because the bread would have been from the wrong source. It's more important where your daily bread comes from than whether you have enough bread.

As the Israelites were ready to enter Canaan, God warned them, "Beware that you do not forget the Lord your God" (Deut. 8:11).

Why We Forget the Source of Our Provision

Why were the Israelites in danger of forgetting God? Because they were going into a good land, and if they weren't careful they would forget that God gave it to them. Then they would start saying, "My power and the strength of my hand made me this wealth" (v. 17).

We can do the same thing. We may remember Him when we are in the apartment or living dollar to dollar, but it's easiest to forget God when things start going well and to start saying,

"Wait a minute. I'm the one making the living here. I built this company with my own hands. I'm the one making the great deals. I've earned everything I have by my own hard work and dedication."

God has a remedy for that kind of spiritual amnesia through His reminder to remember where your success ultimately comes from, "You shall remember the Lord your God, for it is He who is giving you power to make wealth" (v. 18).

Asking God for your daily bread, blessing, favor, and His grace in your life is a great reminder of who your Provider really is. Jesus used bread in the Lord's Prayer example to represent all of our physical needs. He was saying that if we are taking care of God's priorities and concerns, we won't have to worry about our bread. If we are serving God's kingdom, the King will cover our needs.

But what we do so often is let our physical needs get ahead of our spiritual priorities, and we wind up messed up on both counts. When you make bread (the physical life) an end in itself, then your only concern is, "When do we eat?" You don't care too much who provided the bread.

Remember His Provision, Receive His Blessing

Jesus' example in the wilderness teaches us that God is more important than our physical satisfaction. When we find our satisfaction and sustenance in Him, then the promise of Philippians 4:19 kicks in: "God will supply all your needs according to His riches in glory in Christ Jesus."

Notice that Paul said "according to," not "out of." A wealthy person could give you a measly dollar out of his riches. But if he were to give you a gift according to, or in keeping with, his riches, you'd have something special coming.

Recently, I was talking to a businessman who was trying to close a million-dollar deal. He wanted me to pray with him about this deal. I said, "Before we pray, let me ask you a question. If this deal goes through, what does God get out of it?"

> *God has promised to supply our needs when we are putting Him and His kingdom first.*

He started scratching his head and rubbing his eyes because he had not considered that before. You see, when you start praying, "Give me," and God isn't part of the deal, you've got it backwards.

TIMES WHEN GOD MAY NOT PROVIDE OUR NEEDS

God has promised to supply our needs when we are putting Him and His kingdom first (see Matt. 6:33). But there are times when He may not do that. I can think of two situations.

The first is suggested by the conversation I had with that businessman. That is, God may not meet our needs because of our carnality. Like the prodigal son, we may be in a far country eating with the pigs when God is abundantly supplying everyone's needs back home in the Father's house. When we get up and come back home, God will start meeting our needs.

Another occasion when God may not meet our physical needs is when He is testing us to take us to the next spiritual level. The issue here is not whether God will meet a need, but when.

God may have a specific purpose for not responding imme-diately, but David could say confidently, "I have been young and now I am old, yet I have not seen the righteous forsaken or his descendants begging bread" (Psalm 37:25). God the Father has never walked out on His children.

The provision we are taught to pray for is supplied "this day." Jesus emphasized the "dailyness" of God's supply. The best example of this is Israel in the wilderness. The people were hun-gry, so God rained down a white, flaky substance called manna (Ex. 16:13–21). Manna was bread from heaven, and God's in-struction was that the Israelites were to gather only enough for each day. Anything they tried to keep overnight, except for the Sabbath, turned rancid or stale.

A lot of us are living off stale blessings. We haven't hallowed God's name, prioritized His kingdom, or obeyed His will, so by the time we get to our bread, it's stale. Nobody wants stale bread. We want it to be fresh. But we can't enjoy it fresh when we are giving God our stale, leftover service.

Why does God want us to come to Him each day for our needs? Because coming keeps us thankful and dependent. When the refrigerator and freezer are full, it's easy to forget to trust God and not depend on His provision. We need this truth in our culture because most of us have tomorrow's food on hand today.

During my time in seminary, when forced to depend on God in such a practical, everyday sort of way, I found it easier to think of God as my provider. Because I had to. I also found it easier, almost involuntarily, to be grateful for everything we got. Yet the greater test comes when we feel like our needs are met, either through a secure job or savings. It is in those times where the truth of our hearts comes out—do we really depend on God daily? Or is He an afterthought?

ARE WE GRATEFUL FOR HIS GRACE?

And as God provides, are we truly grateful? Or is it just lip service when we thank God for what He has done?

Did you realize giving thanks is actually a decree from God? Prayerful thanksgiving is something we are told to do. Paul writes in 1 Thessalonians 5:18, "In everything give thanks; for this is God's will for you in Christ Jesus." You can't get any more straightforward than that! Scripture specifically spells it out that God's will for you and me is to give thanks. Of course, when you are giving thanks—you are praying. Thus, thanksgiving should be a regular, ongoing, and even organic part of your prayer life. After all, it is a divine expectation.

In fact, the Bible goes so far as to say that it is evil not to thank God. Paul writes, "For even though they knew God, they did not honor Him as God or give thanks, but they became futile in their speculations, and their foolish heart was darkened" (Rom. 1:21). To know God and to know what He has done and has created, and yet to go without saying thank you is one of the most grievous things a person can do. Even so, God is the entity who is the most taken for granted in the universe.

The truth is everything we do is dependent on God. Every breath we take depends on Him to provide the oxygen and to make our lungs work. Everything we have is supplied by a source beyond us. The money in our wallets was printed from the paper from a tree that God made in the ground that He owns. The cars we drive were fitted together from the metal derived from materials God placed in the earth. The gold jewelry we wear around our necks or wrists or fingers is from a deposit God provided.

Scripture says over and over that God is the source of all good things, so we know He doesn't want us to forget that He gave us everything we have. *It is all His.* Yet we are all ungrateful at times, unhappy with what we have and wanting more of what we don't have, and these attitudes prevent us from focusing on God's graciousness.

Two remarkable examples of this ingratitude appear in the Scriptures. One happened during the daily appearance of manna, that bread from heaven mentioned earlier. God sent manna Monday through Friday, and then he sent enough for two days so that the people wouldn't have to collect manna on the Sabbath. God took care of every detail. Yet how did the Israelites respond to God's provision? They complained that they were tired of the manna; they wanted some meat. So God sent them quail to eat—and then they were greedy with it as well (see Num. 11:4–35).

One New Testament account matches the Old Testament as an example of ingratitude. Ten leprous men approached Jesus, "and they raised their voices, saying, 'Jesus, Master, have mercy on us!'" (v. 13) And the Master responded with great kindness:

> When He saw them, He said to them, "Go and show yourselves to the priests." And as they were going, they were cleansed. Now one of them, when he saw that he had been healed, turned back, glorifying God with a loud voice, and he fell on his face at His feet, giving thanks to Him. And he was a Samaritan. Then Jesus answered and said, "Were there not ten cleansed? But the nine—where are they? Was no one found who returned to give glory to God, except this foreigner?" And He said to him, "Stand up and go; your faith has made you well." (Luke 17:14–19)

Jesus healed ten, yet only one bothered to thank Him!

COUNT YOUR BLESSINGS

Take a moment to think about all that God has given to you. Do you truly have a spirit of ongoing gratitude? Or would you say that more often you are thinking about what you want rather than being content with what you already have?

The best antidote for ingratitude is to recognize God's blessings, large and small. When I was growing up in church, we sang a great hymn called "Count Your Blessings." It said, "Count your blessings, name them one by one. Count your blessings, see what God has done." This is such an important principle. When you count your many blessings, it will surprise you how much God has actually done for you. What good things do you enjoy in your life? You might be saying, "I have too many problems to try and focus on any blessings right now." Well, life is always made of good and bad, so shouldn't we try to focus on the good? Sure, you may have one or two big, looming problems, but think about the many little everyday gifts God sends your way.

THE CONTEXT OF GIVING THANKS

As we saw earlier, 1 Thessalonians 5:18 commands us to be thankful *in everything*. Notice that Paul does not say, "Be thankful *for* everything." There is a distinct difference. He says to give thanks *in* everything. When things go wrong, we are supposed to give thanks to God in the midst of the trouble.

The Words of Habakkuk:
Praising God in the Midst of Circumstances

One of the most poetic passages in Scripture is Habakkuk 3:17–19. It describes how Habakkuk would regard God even if everything in his fields and among his flocks would perish. The prophet wrote:

> Though the fig tree should not blossom
> And there be no fruit on the vines,
> Though the yield of the olive should fail
> And the fields produce no food,
> Though the flock should be cut off from the fold
> And there be no cattle in the stalls,
> Yet I will exult in the Lord,
> I will rejoice in the God of my salvation.
> The Lord God is my strength,
> And He has made my feet like hinds' feet,
> And makes me walk on my high places.

Friend, even though all your worldly efforts and pursuits may fail, even though you may have nothing to your name, and even if you are in the worst season of life, you just still praise God for all He has done. Even though you can't praise God *for* your circumstances, you can praise God that He is with you *in* those circumstances.

The Words of Job:
Blessing God for Ruling over His Life

Do you remember what Job says when he finds his whole life collapsing around him? His wife tells him to curse God. But Job says: "You speak as one of the foolish women speaks. Should we indeed accept good from God and not accept adversity?" (Job 2:10). Job is saying that we can't measure our relationship with God by the good things He gives us. Job says, "The Lord gave and the Lord has taken away. Blessed be the name of the Lord" (Job 1:21).

Job praises God even at the lowest point in his life. He has lost his children, job, workers, income, health—everything has gone wrong for him. So why does he thank God? Because Job knows that you can't lose what wasn't really yours to begin with. Job understands that all he had belonged to the Lord, and he recognizes that God is supreme over all of his life.

God can give and take because He is in control, and Job trusts that fact.

The Words of Jehosophat:
Praise for God's Mighty Power

Another example of praising God in everything and what it can ultimately produce is found in 2 Chronicles 20. King Jehosophat chose to praise God even when he felt powerless in a defeated situation. Then he said, "Our God, will You not judge them? For we are powerless before this great multitude who are coming against us. . . . We do not know what to do" (v.12).

Jehoshaphat did not know what to do. He had nothing to thank God for, at least with regard to the battle he faced. And at least not from a human perspective. But let's take a look at what he did do and apply the king's response to our own situation of prayer. Jehosophat used his lips for praise to gain the victory he sought. What an interesting battle strategy. This king fought (and won) his war in prayer:

"Yahweh, the God of our ancestors, are You not the God who is in heaven, and do You not rule over all the kingdoms of the nations? Power and might are in Your hand, and no one can stand against You. Are You not our God who drove out the inhabitants of this land before Your people Israel and who gave it forever to the descendants of Abraham Your friend? They have lived in the land and have built You a sanctuary in it for Your name and have said, 'If disaster comes on us—sword or judgment, pestilence or famine—we will stand before this temple and before You, for Your name is in this temple. We will cry out to You because of our distress, and You will hear and deliver.'" (2 Chron. 20:6–9)

Let's look at the anatomy of the king's prayer to help us in our own prayers. First, he began by reminding God who He is. The king praised God for the "power and might . . . in [His] hand." Then he reminded God about what He had said. Following that, he told God about the issue at hand.

The order of his prayer matters, so read that paragraph again. It puts things in the right perspective. When you or I face a big problem in our lives, it means we need something that can give us a bigger solution—that something is God.

You will never discover that God is all you need until God is all you have. There are times in your life when God will allow you to be overwhelmed so you can have a bigger view of Him. See, if your view of God is small than He will be the last resort you turn to in a difficult situation. You won't really expect too much from Him. But if your view of God is great—as was the king's—you will turn to Him to deliver you, and you will begin by reminding Him of His greatness.

King Jehosophat had no doubt experienced numbers of successes in his reign but at the time of this battle, he was facing a crisis that revealed his own weaknesses. That's why he used prayer to call on God. Sometimes you are in a ditch in a bus that you cannot get out of, but if Clark Kent is on the same bus—it changes your strategy. In prayer, remind God of His greatness, power and strength and His willingness to help you when you are in trouble. Ahead of time Jehosophat understood that like a basketball player palms a ball, God has the universe in His control. His faith was like that of Linda (chap. 10), who prayed beneath a football stadium that the God who "can control the weather" would intercede to divert a huge thunderstorm that threatened a meeting to proclaim the gospel and to jeopardize God's good name.

In verse 15 of the passage, we read God's response to all the people through His prophet. It says, "Listen carefully, all Judah and you inhabitants of Jerusalem, and King Jehoshaphat. This is what the Lord says: 'Do not be afraid or discouraged because of this vast number, for the battle is not yours, but God's.'"

In other words, this battle belongs to the Lord.

The prophet came and declared God's specific instruction. He told the Israelites that in this particular battle, they would not need to fight. In this battle, all the Israelites needed to do the next day, as recorded in 2 Chronicles 20, was:

> "'Go down against them. You will see them coming up the Ascent of Ziz, and you will find them at the end of the valley facing the Wilderness of Jeruel. You need not fight in this battle; station yourselves, stand and see the salvation of the Lord on your behalf, O Judah and Jerusalem.' Do not fear or be dismayed; tomorrow go out to face them, for the Lord is with you." (vv. 16–17)

They just had to stand still. As a result of hearing this, Jehosophat "bowed with his face to the ground, and all Judah and the inhabitants of Jerusalem fell down before the Lord, worshiping the Lord" (v. 18). In fact, they began to praise God with a very loud voice. The Scripture continues, "The Levites, from the sons of the Kohathites and of the sons of the Korahites, stood up to praise the Lord God of Israel, with a very loud voice" (v. 19).

The next morning they woke up and praised all over again in anticipation of victory. We read,

> They rose early in the morning and went out to the wilderness of Tekoa; and when they went out, Jehoshaphat stood and said, "Listen to me, O Judah and inhabitants of Jerusalem, put your trust in the Lord your God and you will be established. Put your trust in His prophets and succeed." When he had consulted with the people, he appointed those who sang to the Lord and those who praised Him in holy attire, as they went out before the army and said, "Give thanks to the Lord, for His lovingkindness is everlasting." (vv. 20–21)

When the Israelites began singing, thanking God and praising God, God set ambushes against their enemies (vv. 22–23). In response to their thanksgiving, the Lord got the job done for them.

GIVE PRAISE AND THANKS
AS AN ACT OF SACRIFICE

Friend, never allow yourself to be too cute or too sophisticated to praise and thank God. Give God the delight of experiencing your trust in Him through your prayerful thanksgiving. Let praise and thanksgiving continually be in your heart and on your lips as you give God the glory that is due Him.

And when times are down and struggles are tough, you can

still thank Him. Let your praise and thanksgiving be a *sacrifice*, as it is called in the book of Hebrews 13:15. Sometimes it is more difficult to see the good in a situation just as it was for the Israelites when their enemies surrounded them. It is in those times that offering praise and thanksgiving is truly a sacrifice. You are praising and thanking Him in faith despite the pain and confusion around you. When you do, it is especially in those times that the Lord hears your heart and rewards the authenticity of your praise with His presence.

When the Israelites chose to give God praise and thanksgiving in obedience and in faith during their battle, they received the victory they were promised. So tied is the victory to their thanksgiving that the Scripture makes a point of giving us the exact timing that each took place. In fact, it was precisely when God heard their praise, that they received His hand of intervention in their war. Not a moment before. Not even a moment after. God synchronized His deliverance with their prayer of praise and thanksgiving: As they began to sing and praise, "the Lord set ambushes against [those] who had come against Judah; so they were routed" (2 Chron. 20:22–23). The moment they began their shouts and praises, the Lord set ambushes against those who came to fight against Judah, and they were defeated.

Friend, don't delay. Give the King kingdom praise. Praise and thank God now, ahead of the time, demonstrating your trust in His divine ability to overturn whatever situation you may be facing.

When you give thanks, you are in the will of God. When you are grumbling, you are outside of God's will. To give thanks is to position yourself smack-dab in the middle of God's will. This is critical because "We know that God causes all things to work together for good to those who love God, to those who are called according to His purpose" (Rom. 8:28). We know beyond doubt that God is working out His will in the lives of believers, and He is using the tough times for a purpose.

As finite creatures, we find it hard to see the big picture; we tend to see only a piece here and a piece there. But our Father sees the whole picture and how everything interconnects. He is stitching all the pieces together so that all things work together in the process of accomplishing His kingdom agenda.

Don't just take my word for it. Take His. Test Him, and make gratitude a regular part of your thoughts, words, and prayers.

CHAPTER 16

Breaking Free from Bondage

There are times in our lives where the trouble we are in is of our own doing. We made mistakes. We made wrong choices. We brought the consequence on ourselves.

That's a challenging bondage and weight to live under. But then there are also those times when what we are facing has nothing to do with anything we may have done wrong. In fact, we may have even done something right—and as a result, we face difficulties.

As an example, the disciples in the boat on the Sea of Galilee were obeying Jesus when they were caught in the middle of a raging storm. They hadn't done anything wrong to deserve the difficulty they were facing. Their obedience led to great danger. At times God allows these challenges to test us or strengthen us. Other times it is Satan seeking to devour us. Scripture tells us that no weapon formed against us will prosper (Isa. 54:17), but it never says the weapons won't form. To live in light of this reality means we must have a mental strategy for when we face life's challenges.

FACING THE ADVERSARY

We have an adversary and his name is Satan. He is in the discouragement business and every opportunity to bring us emotionally or psychologically to our knees serves his ultimate purpose: separating us from God emotionally, spiritually, and mentally.

Matthew's gospel records the story of Peter walking on water, brimming with faith that Jesus would keep him from sinking, even in the middle of an awful storm. Peter said to Jesus, "Lord, if it is You, command me to come to You on the water," to which Jesus said, "Come" (Matt. 14:28–29). Yet, even in the middle of a bona fide miracle, Peter could not help but be frightened by a ferocious wind. Even during an act of courageous obedience, Satan delivered discouragement to the fisherman, who began to sink.

Think about all the sinking moments in your life. Lost jobs, quarrels with family, bad report from the doctor. Each of us has tasted that despair, fear, worry, or hopelessness. If we're honest, it is in those moments that we feel as though God is far off. And that He does not care.

But the Bible commands us to draw near to Him and to resist the devil, who *will* flee from us (James 4:7–8). As believers, we easily forget that we have been empowered to do that which God has commanded, just like Peter, who was first commanded to walk out on the water.

Unbelief comes as quickly as it goes and when the winds of life blow hard against our bow, it has a way of discouraging even the most faithful among us. But, if we keep our eyes on Christ—follow His teachings and pray as He taught us—we will be able to weather the fiercest of storms or the darkest of nights.

ADMITTING OUR DOUBTS

As Peter began to sink underneath the water, his prayer wasn't long, eloquent, or even well thought out. Essentially, he called out for help: "Lord, save me." Three words. Not exactly something to write home about. But it was effective. Sometimes our prayers don't need to be nearly as long as we make them. Remember, God listens to our hearts. If you need help in a challenging situation, ask for it. If you doubt God because of the circumstances surrounding you, ask Him to help your unbelief turn into belief (Mark 9:24). If you need confirmation, request it. When you need comfort, say it.

As a husband, I can stand with many husbands who have discovered over the years that our wives sometimes expect us to read their minds. You may get home from work and the reception be as cold as the ice cap of the North Pole, but when you ask what is wrong, you hear, "Nothing is wrong." You sigh, knowing that thus begins the hard work of seeking to chisel through that ice to uncover what is wrong. Many of us do the same with God. Either we are too afraid that He won't like what we have to say or we doubt that He will address us, so we are protecting our own hopes and expectations. Whatever the case, far too many believers tell God what is wrong and ask Him to address it. We live under the umbrella of trying to be a "super saint" when inside we are crumbling from doubt, worry, and even disappointment.

WHEN YOU'RE IN A DEEP HOLE

An important principle in kingdom prayer is always this: Be honest with God—after all, He knows how you feel already. Tell

Him. Start the conversation. Even if it's as simple as Peter's cry, "Lord, save me," go ahead and say it. You may feel alone but you are not alone. When God is silent, He is not still. Even in the darkest of nights and deepest of pits, He is there.

There is an old story about a man who has fallen in a hole and sees no way out. He hollers for help, and eventually a rugged man approaches. Upon hearing the man's plea and seeing his predicament, the hiker tells the man that he needs to pick himself up by the bootstraps and find a way out on his own, before going on his way. A holy man walks by and hears the man's desperate cry. He tells him that he will say a prayer for him that he will find his way out and then scurries off.

Finally, an ordinary man walks by the hole and sees the first man and his situation. He listens to the man's plea for help. Then, without warning, the ordinary man jumps down into the hole with the first man. "Why did you do that?" the first man asks. The ordinary man replies, "Because I have been in this hole before, and I know the way out."

Jesus Christ is such a man. Jesus is the Son of the living God, but He is also God Himself. Yet, in John 1:14, we find out that this Son of God came down to Earth and became a man and lived among the human race. He "emptied Himself" of the independent use of His deity and assumed the mortality of humans, to include the frustration of temptation and the anguish of death itself. Why? So we would have a true advocate interceding for us forever, One who fully understands what we go through and One who knows the way out.

If you feel as though you have fallen in a hole, suffering through some trial to which you see no way out, take heart that an Advocate is interceding on your behalf. He knows exactly what you're going through and is committed to seeing you climb out of that hole. And there is a strategy He has given to us on how we are to respond in situations like that. We discover this in a story found in Acts 16.

Paul and Silas in a Deep Hole

Paul and Silas had been displaying the power of God in Rome by healing people, casting out demons, and leading people to Christ through conversion. They were living in obedience to God. Their success upset some of the businessmen in the city. After all, one of the demons that these two disciples had cast out left a girl who "divined" for a profit. The businessmen made money from her ability to tell futures and cast spells.

After enough complaints came in, the two men were harshly accused, beaten badly and then thrown into the inner prison and bound in chains, having their feet fastened in stocks. Locked down. This prison represented the worst possible situation. It was dirty. They were isolated. Based on accusations against both race and religion, the two men were locked up with no trial in sight.

And what do you think they did while in this deep hole? They did something few of us would have done. But what all of us should do. They prayed, and they praised. Verse 25 says, "But about midnight Paul and Silas were praying and singing hymns of praise to God, and the prisoners were listening to them." Notice that they were praying and praising at "about midnight"! I always get excited when I read or hear "about midnight." You should too. Typically when it's included, it means in the worst of times—the darkest of times—the most hopeless of times. And yet God's going to turn it around.

About midnight, Paul and Silas were not cussing, complaining, or asking why. They weren't debating whether they had heard their calling correctly. In the inner prison of the prisons, locked down with feet in chains—for no reason other than following God and serving Him publicly through healing and helping others—Paul and Silas were praying and praising.

That is exactly what we are supposed to be doing when we find ourselves in an "about midnight" kind of situation. Maybe they remembered these words from the Scriptures:

> But no one says, "Where is God my Maker, Who gives songs in the night?" (Job 35:10)

> The Lord will command His lovingkindness in the daytime; and His song will be with me in the night, a prayer to the God of my life. (Ps. 42:8)

Whatever the case, they chose to sing in the moment when most would have questioned God and said things just weren't fair. Asking God questions is what we sometimes do when life gets dark and there seems to be no way out of an unfair situation. At such times, when you want to give up or just rot all alone in self-pity, God says you are to get your praise on. This is because the worse off you are, the more you need God.

Praise and Prayer Depends on Our View of God

How we respond in suffering is directly related to our view of God. How we react at midnight (not at noon when the sun is bright) has everything to do with our concept of God. When midnight comes, and all of us will have a midnight or two or more, what we truly believe about God comes out.

When depression covers you like a cloud, or anxiety wraps its ugly chains around your lungs or the bills pile so high you can't see over, it is the time to praise and pray—in faith. God responds to the prayer and praises of His people, especially at midnight. Such prayer and praise reflects the truth Paul would write about in Romans: "All things work together for good to those who love God and are called according to His purpose" (8:28). Even those things we can't understand work together for good.

Paul and Silas weren't praising God for the prison. They were praising Him for the purpose. When you are in a bad situation and it's about midnight in your life, you are not called to praise God for the pain but to thank Him for the greater purpose He is bringing about. A heart of prayer, praise, and gratitude in our darkest moments of life demonstrates faith like nothing else. And ushers in a response you could never have predicted or thought up yourself.

Praise is the switch that turned on the power of God. Praise gets God to do the unexpected, unpredictable, the "out of nowhere"—the *suddenly*.

PRAISE AND THE SUDDENLY

Acts 16:26 contains some of the most powerful spiritual truths with regard to kingdom prayer. It says, "and suddenly there came a great earthquake, so that the foundations of the prison house were shaken; and immediately all the doors were opened and everyone's chains were unfastened." Not only did this great earthquake come immediately—but it also unfastened everyone's chains. Who has ever heard of an earthquake unfastening chains? God shook things up in such a way that the doors opened and all of the prisoners were set free.

Keep in mind, it happened suddenly. No one can see suddenly coming. That's what makes it suddenly. You can't hear it approaching or see the signs that it is near. If you are trusting God but when you look for His hand and see nothing, remember that God often works suddenly. You aren't going to see what He's doing until He is ready to reveal it. All you need to be responsible for is you. Let God handle the suddenly. All Paul and Silas needed to do was pray and praise in the midst of a midnight kind of dilemma. As a result, God set them free.

Yet the two men did not walk out of the prison. Instead they sought to save the jailor on watch. He feared for his own life since he assumed the prisoners had escaped. Seeing that the jailor was going to kill himself, Paul cried out with a loud voice and told him not to harm himself because all the prisoners were still there. Even in their freedom and in their blessings, Paul was faithful to what God had asked him to do. And he led the other prisoners on the same path. As a result, the jailer and his entire household later became Christians as well (vv. 27–34).

Things had gone from bad to worse for Paul and Silas. First they were accused wrongly; then they were beaten, put in jail, and bound securely. But despite the negative situation surrounding them, they sang back to God to give Him glory. Praise reminds us that no chain is too thick that God cannot break it—suddenly.

Joshua and his army must have hit the right pitch in their praise when they circled Jericho because the walls shattered and came tumbling down. Jehoshaphat and his army hit the same pitch of praise when they sang and God went ahead of them to defeat the enemy in battle by confusing them.

You know a rooster sings only when the sun comes up. The robin sings only during the day when it is trying to impress a member of the opposite sex. But a nightingale sings all day long. Which kind of bird are you? Do you only sing when the sun is up? Or do you only sing when you want something? Or, rather, is sending up your praise just the way you are—no matter if it's morning or midnight?

Make prayer and praise your modus operandi, your normal way of approaching situations in life, and you will be opening yourself up to experience a world full of *suddenlies*. Expect earthquakes when you pray. Expect walls tumbling down. Expect chains falling off.

Expect miracles, suddenly. He *is* able, according to the power working *in you*.

True Power

D o you remember my family's visit to Niagara Falls, high-
lighted in chapter 1? We began by looking out a hotel window a couple of blocks from those mighty falls. Then we walked
right up to the overlook. Others decided to board the Maid of
the Mist to get as close as humanly possible to admire—and
fear—its mighty power.

You too can either observe or participate in those mighty
falls. The easiest way is to view a calendar photo featuring the
Falls. Or you can participate, but the question is, "How much?"
You can travel to the general area of the Falls and look out a
hotel window. Even better, you could choose to walk down to
the park and line up at the edge where the water rushes over the
top. *Or* you will decide to go all the way—put on the raincoat,
get on the boat, and be drenched by the power of that place.

When it comes to the mighty power of kingdom prayer you
also have a choice. But remember, the choice you make affects
the outcome. If you want the full power and promises of God's
presence, you will have *to get close and go deep in your relationship with Him.*

This book is a study of how we can tap into the power of kingdom prayer, which is *the divinely authorized methodology to access heavenly authority for earthly intervention*. Beginning with your relationship with God the Father and God the Son, keep these truths in mind as you pray in Jesus' name for His kingdom purposes:

1. Draw close to God's Son, giving Jesus Christ access to and rule over every place of your life. Practice this lordship of Jesus every day so you might hear His voice and honor His kingdom.

2. Prayer is relational communication with God. Be sincere, direct, and honest in your prayers.

3. Your Father in heaven is in charge. He is sovereign over all, which means He has the power and wisdom to answer our prayers in the right way at the right time.

4. Pray often (1 Thess. 5:16), and listen for His response.

5. Pray specifically, persistently, and expectantly.

6. Your prayers should benefit others, bring glory to God, and advance God's kingdom agenda.

7. Solitude allows you to hear God's supernatural voice.

8. Effective prayer requires obedience.

9. Have a growing faith (the size of a mustard seed) so God may answer your prayers. Unbelief limits what God will do in and through your life.

10. Consider fasting at times of crisis. By fasting, you deliberately show God that you are serious about getting His attention, and you can listen intently for His voice.

Choose today to get involved with God in prayer—to know Him and obey Him, to hear His voice, and to draw near to His Son. Pray in order to benefit others, bring glory to God, and advance God's kingdom agenda. Do this, and you will see how touching heaven can change earth.

Notes

Chapter 1: Power and Promises

1. Calculations are based on the sun's average distance from earth being ninety-three million miles and the speed of light traveling at 186,000 miles per second. See "How Far Away Is the Sun?"; http://coolcosmos.ipac.caltech.edu/ask/8-How-far-away-is-the-Sun-

Chapter 3: Ruling and Relationship

1. Quentin Fottrell, "$750M in Gift Cards Will Go Unused in 2014," New York Post, November 29, 2014, http://nypost.com/2014/11/29/750-million-in-gift-cards-will-go-unused-in-2014; originally published by MarketWatch, December 1, 2014, http://www.marketwatch.com/story/750-million-in-gift-cards-will-go-unused-in-2014-2014-11-29.

Chapter 6: Faith and Futility

1. Dominique Mosbergen, "This Inspiring Runner Took a Nasty Fall But She Didn't Stay Down," *The Huffington Post*, May 27, 2014; http://www.huffingtonpost.com/2014/05/27/; runner-falls-wins-race-heather-dorniden_n_5395232.html
2. As of this writing, the video of her race has received 14.7 million views on YouTube both in the United States and overseas.
3. Rick Moore, "Big Fish, Big Pond," University of Minnesota, May 13, 2009, reprint June 5, 2009, "Heather Dorniden: The Runner Who Didn't Give Up," http://nhne-pulse.org/heather-dorniden-the-runner-who-didnt-give-up/
4. The IAFF, or International Association of Athletics Federations, was founded in 1912 in Stockholm, Sweden following the closing ceremony of the Olympic Games in the country. Its original name was the International Amateur Athletic Federation.
5. Heather Kampf, "Monday in Minnesota—Tuesday in Poland," Heather Kampf (blog), March 5, 2014; http://goheatherkampf.com/blog/monday-in-minnesota-tuesday-poland

Chapter 7: Two or Three Together

1. Lee Moran, "Marine Runs Alongside Boy Struggling to Finish 5k Race," *New York Daily News*, August 2, 2013, http://www.nydailynews.com/news/national/marine-runs-boy-struggling-finish-5k-race-article-1.1415589

2. Sasha Goldstein, "High School Runner Carries Rival across Finish Line at North Dakota cross-country," *New York Daily News*, October 17, 2014, http://www.nydailynews.com/ sports/high-school-runner-carries-rival-finish-line-cross-country-race-article-1.1978574

Chapter 11: Making Mountains Move

1. Two parallel passages reveal the boy was demon possessed. See Mark 9:17–21, 25–29 and Luke 9:37–42.

The Urban Alternative

D r. Tony evans and The Urban Alternative (TUA) **equips, empowers**, and **unites** Christians to **impact** *individuals, families, churches*, and *communities* to restore hope and transform lives..

We believe the core cause of the problems we face in our personal lives, homes, churches, and societies is a spiritual one; therefore, the only way to address them is spiritually. We've tried a political, a social, an economic, and even a religious agenda. It's time for a Kingdom Agenda—God's visible and comprehensive rule over every area of life because when we function as we were designed, there is a divine power that changes everything. It renews and restores as the life of Christ is made manifest within our own. As we align ourselves under Him, there is an alignment that happens from deep within— where He brings about full restoration. It is an atmosphere that revives and makes whole.

As it impacts us, it impacts others—transforming every sphere of life in which we live. When each biblical sphere of life functions in accordance with God's Word, the outcomes are evangelism, discipleship, and community impact. As we learn how to govern ourselves under God, we then transform the institutions of family, church, and society from a biblically based kingdom perspective, where through Him, we are touching heaven and changing earth.

To achieve our goal we use a variety of strategies, methods, and resources for reaching and equipping as many people as possible.

BROADCAST MEDIA

Hundreds of thousands of individuals experience *The Alternative with Dr. Tony Evans* through the daily radio broadcast playing on nearly one thousand radio outlets in more than one hundred countries. The broadcast can also be seen on several television networks, and is viewable online at TonyEvans.org.

LEADERSHIP TRAINING

The Kingdom Agenda Pastors (KAP) provides a *viable network* for like-minded pastors who embrace the Kingdom Agenda philosophy. Pastors have the opportunity to go deeper with Dr. Tony Evans as they are given greater biblical knowledge, practical applications, and resources to impact individuals, families, churches, and communities. KAP welcomes senior and associate pastors of all churches.

The Kingdom Agenda Pastors' Summit progressively develops church leaders to meet the demands of the twenty-first century while maintaining the gospel message and the strategic position of the church. The Summit introduces *intensive seminars, workshops,* and *resources,* addressing issues affecting the community, family, leadership, organizational health, and more.

Pastors' Wives Ministry, founded by Dr. Lois Evans, provides *counsel, encouragement,* and *spiritual resources* for pastors' wives as they serve with their husbands in the ministry. A primary focus of the ministry is the KAP Summit that offers senior pastors' wives a safe place to *reflect, renew,* and *relax* along with training in personal development, spiritual growth, and care for their emotional and physical well-being.

COMMUNITY IMPACT

National Church Adopt-A-School Initiative (NCAASI) prepares churches across the country to impact communities by using *public schools as the primary vehicle for effecting positive social change* in urban youth and families. Leaders of churches, school districts, faith-based organizations, and other non-profit organizations are equipped with the knowledge and tools to *forge partnerships* and build *strong social service delivery systems.* This training is based on the comprehensive church-based community impact strategy conducted by Oak Cliff Bible Fellowship. It addresses such areas as economic development, education, housing, health revitalization, family renewal, and racial reconciliation. We also assist churches in tailoring the model to meet the specific needs of their communities while simultaneously addressing the spiritual and moral frame of reference.

RESOURCE DEVELOPMENT

We are fostering lifelong learning partnerships with the people we serve by providing a variety of published materials. We offer booklets, Bible studies, books, CDs, and DVDs to strengthen people in their walk with God and ministry to others.

* * *

For more information, a catalog of Dr. Tony Evans'
ministry resources, and a complimentary copy of Dr. Evans'
devotional newsletter, call
(800) 800-3222
or write TUA at P.O. Box 4000, Dallas TX 75208,
or log on to
www.TonyEvans.org

THE KINGDOM AGENDA

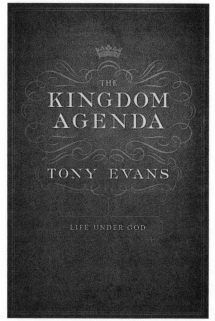

978-0-8024-1061-0

God's kingdom isn't just about theology and church. It isn't just a quaint religious idea or an obscure theological concept. It is about a whole new way of seeing the world and your place in it. As God's people, we are not limited by the choices this world offers us. God has an alternative plan for us— His kingdom with an all-encompassing agenda.

The Kingdom Agenda offers a fresh and powerful vision that will help you think differently about your life, your relationships, and your walk with God. When you start with a kingdom agenda, living in relationship with the true King and embracing your place in His Kingdom, nothing will ever be the same.

MOODY
Publishers™

From the Word to Life

EVANS
THE URBAN ALTERNATIVE

At The Urban Alternative, the national ministry of Dr. Tony Evans, we seek to restore hope and transform lives to reflect the values of the kingdom of God. Along with our community outreach initiative, leadership training and family and personal growth emphasis, Dr. Evans continues to minister to people from the pulpit to the heart as the relevant expositor with the powerful voice. Lives are touched both locally and abroad through our daily radio broadcast, weekly television ministry and internet access points.

PRESENTING AN
ALTERNATIVE TO:

COMMUNITY OUTREACH

Equipping leaders to engage public schools and communities with mentoring, family support services and a commitment to a brighter tomorrow.

LEADERSHIP TRAINING

Offering an exclusive opportunity for pastors and their wives to receive discipleship from Drs. Tony and Lois Evans and the TUA staff, along with networking opportunities, resources and encouragement.

FAMILY AND PERSONAL GROWTH

Strengthening homes and deepening spiritual lives through helpful resources that encourage hope and health for the glory of God.

TONYEVANS.ORG